B. Marian Brooks

AMERICAN
EDUCATION
UNDER FIRE

AMERICAN EDUCATION UNDER FIRE

V. T. THAYER

*Educational Director of the Ethical Culture
Schools; Leader of the Society for Ethical Culture, New York City; Formerly Chairman
of the Commission on the Secondary School Curriculum of the Progressive Education Association*

HARPER & BROTHERS PUBLISHERS

NEW YORK AND LONDON

Contents

Preface

THE American of today is engaged in a profound searching of his soul. The depression and the war have caused him to question the values he lives by. It is natural therefore that he should subject his school to a similar critical examination, since our schools and colleges reflect as well as determine prevailing conceptions of the good life. Ultimately the issues of education are one with the issues of life.

This book attempts to deal with certain crucial issues that confront the citizen as well as the professional educator. Part I examines conflicting theories and trends in American democracy and their implications for education. It concludes with a positive statement of a free man's faith. Part II deals more specifically with a number of controversial problems that have engaged the attention of laymen and educators alike. This section of the book also concludes on a positive note with a broad outline of the task of the modern school.

Portions of several chapters include material which I have published elsewhere in article form; in *The Educational Record*, *The Standard*, a publication of the American Ethical Union, *Frontiers of Democracy*, and *School and Home*, a magazine put forth by the Parents and Teachers Association of the Ethical Culture Schools. The chapter on "Religion and the Public Schools" appeared in *Harper's Magazine* for April, 1944. "Should Communists and Fascists Teach in the Schools?" was printed originally in the *Harvard Educational Review*, but has been revised for inclusion in this volume. Recent developments in the program of the Communist Party would render the discussion of this chapter irrelevant were not the principles involved applicable to all groups that seek to use the schools for their own ends. The role played by the Communists in recent years will undoubtedly be repeated by other groups in the future. The principles at issue thus merit serious consideration.

The author wishes to express his indebtedness to Dorothy Wilson Favreau for her assistance in the preparation of the manuscript as well as for her careful reading and helpful criticisms of it.

V. T. THAYER

New York City
April 1944

AMERICAN
EDUCATION
UNDER FIRE

PART 1

*

CHAPTER I

The Lion and the Lamb
in American Democracy

SOME years ago a message was found in the steeple knob of the church of Saint Margaret in Gotha, Germany. Written in 1784 and addressed to posterity, it reads in part as follows:

Our age occupies the happiest period of the eighteenth century. . . . Sectarian hatred and persecution for conscience' sake are vanishing. Love of man and freedom of thought are gaining the supremacy. The arts and sciences are flourishing, and our gaze is penetrating deeply into the workshop of nature. Handicraftsmen as well as artists are reaching perfection, useful knowledge is growing among all classes. Here you have a faithful description of our times. Do not haughtily look down upon us if you are higher and see farther than we; recognize rather from the picture which we have drawn how bravely and energetically we laboured to raise you to the position which you now hold and to support you in it. Do the same for your descendants and be happy.

Let us examine the basis of this optimistic outlook and its essential characteristics. It emerged out of a profound economic revolution of several centuries' duration, a revolution that witnessed the disintegration of the medieval order based upon control of land, with class lines rigidly defined, and culminated in the domination of society by groups who derived their influence from movable capital—the traders, manufacturers, bankers. Were we to trace even in outline these changes, we should review the profound effects upon European society resulting from discoveries and explorations of the fifteenth and sixteenth centuries, the colonizations of the sixteenth and seventeenth centuries, the expansion in

1

trade following the economic exploitation of virgin conti-
nents, concluding with the imperialistic developments of the
nineteenth and the twentieth centuries. Such a survey would
also deal with the effects of science upon living; the practical
applications of science to the refinements of daily life, of
course; but, even more important, the transformation of ways
of thinking that derived from science; the change in accepted
methods of arriving at truth; the secularization of thought.

Nor should this account ignore the peculiar blend given
to liberalism by life on the American frontier. For a short
time only was there anything analogous to a landed aristoc-
racy, or an upper class in American society. No permanent
upper class has retarded the economic revolution to which
we refer, and virtually no submerged class constituted in this
country a group apart from the middle class. On the contrary,
in America, practically the entire population quickly identified itself with the middle classes, and middle-class philosophy
early permeated society as a whole. Conditions on the frontier were friendly to the ideal of judging men in terms of
what they can do, what they *are*, rather than on the basis of
origin or inherited status. That is to say, the American frontier speeded up on this continent an economic and social
revolution that came about more slowly in Europe.

II

What points of view regarding man and his society were
promoted by this revolution?

First is the idea of the individual as a self-sustaining unit
and the state as an instrument to this end. In Europe individualism evolved slowly out of a background of authoritarianism. It lacked a frontier to soften its crudest expressions
and to give it convincing demonstration. In this country, on
the other hand, experience seemed to confirm the existence
of a state of nature in which man existed prior to organized
society.

The American frontiersman conceived of man as a self-sustaining individual and the state, if not hostile to his purposes, as an instrument serving at best a minimum of his needs. Well might this conception ring true for people who had moved to the frontier as individuals, or in family groups, and had confronted there the stern necessity of organizing a civil community. To them the facts of experience seemed to demonstrate that man antedates his society.

The material conditions and opportunities of American life gave a unique flavor to American individualism. But our religious and philosophical backgrounds also contributed to isolate man from his fellows and to generate in him the idea of government as an unfriendly alien.

Many people came to this country as members of religious groups seeking to build here a way of life in harmony with the Bible as they read it. They quickly established schools for the specific purpose of enabling each person to read and interpret the Bible for himself; to determine his own way of salvation. This way of salvation, however, was an individual matter between a man and his God. Each saved his soul by following what seemed to him the true interpretation of the Bible.

This individualistic emphasis in American religious life confirmed the isolation of the individual and his independence of civil government. It prompted men to segregate the inner motives determining their behavior from their relations with others. Parrington cites, as an example of this religious antagonism to government, a comment of a writer in the *Dial* of 1841 relative to the establishment of a Universalist sect in New England. The writer insists that "a true community can be founded on nothing short of faith in the universal man, as he comes from the hands of the Creator, with no law over his liberty, but the eternal ideas that lie at the foundation of his being."[1]

Emerson and the Transcendentalists helped to perpetuate

[1] *Main Currents in American Thought*, Vol. II, p. 348. New York: Harcourt Brace and Co., 1927.

this suspicion of man-made government and a faith that the inner nature of people can alone lead them into harmonious relations with their neighbors. Accordingly Emerson wrote in his essay *On Politics*[2] that "Every state is corrupt. Good men must not obey the laws too well." And again, "That which all things tend to educe, which freedom, cultivation, intercourse, revolutions, go to form and deliver, is character; that is the end of nature, to reach into this coronation of her king. To educate the wise man, the State exists; and with the appearance of the wise man, the State expires."

American society has changed profoundly since Emerson. Nevertheless the attitudes described still persist to influence men's minds and men's actions. Organized society, particularly government, they would still subordinate to the individual. Its nature they conceive as bad. Politics is in disrepute and the man of character holds himself aloof from public office. Since little of good can flow from what is essentially evil, the American believes, with Jefferson, that the best government is one that governs least.

This individualistic concept of the relation of the individual to government determines also our notions of relations between states. As a young nation we had every reason to follow Washington's advice and to refrain from entangling alliances. Isolation thus became a first principle of international policy. But what is isolation so conceived other than the idea of *laissez faire* transferred to international politics? Americans have believed, in common with other nations, that just as the individual contributes best to the group by pursuing his own self-interests, so nations contribute most wisely to society as a whole by adhering to their national self-interests. This, too, is an inherent element in our tradition.

How do people arrive at decisions individually or as members of self-contained groups?

By the processes of reason. It was assumed that man is gov-

[2] *The Prose Works of Ralph Waldo Emerson*, Vol. I, p. 529. Boston: Fields, Osgood and Co., 1870.

erned by reason. John Stuart Mill, the philosopher of English individualism, based his concept of liberty on the idea of man as a rational being. This was an aristocratic notion, since Mill contended that ninety-nine people out of a hundred are incapable of arriving at wise decisions when confronted by complex questions. Reason, however, can safeguard them from error since it is to the faculty of reason that the hundredth man, who discerns the truth, can appeal. Men benefit from the contributions of the rare individual, however, only when they keep open the channels to truth: appeal to facts, open discussion, freedom of assembly. Just as the individual determines the truth by forcing himself to maintain an open mind and to consider all relevant data and every possible hypothesis, so society as a whole arrives at wise decisions by an analogous procedure.

The concept of man as uniquely a reasoning animal, and the companion principle that truth emerges from the minority, early became an axiom in America. We have long believed with Emerson, that "whoso would be a man must be a non-conformist." We feel that the minority of today is certain to become the majority of tomorrow. This happens on occasion, but Americans are likely to conclude it follows automatically.

Finally, the American, traditionally, is an optimist. His faith presupposes an ability on the part of people, if they so will, to improve their economic status. For generations men have laid their plans on the assumption of an open road ahead.

Democracy in America has kept step with the exploitation of a continent. Jacksonian democracy reflected our westward expansion and a faith in people peculiar to men who were busy creating out of its natural wealth attractive futures for themselves and their children. Following the Civil War and the period characterized by the Beards as our Gilded Age, new possibilities of well-being seemed to flow increasingly from mine and factory and market place.

This atmosphere of economic promise has influenced the

attitudes of the American toward himself and others. On the one hand he is friendly, willing to extend a helping hand to the stranger, on occasion, even, to aid his competitor. On the other hand, he is crudely indifferent to the effects of his action upon the fate of his fellows. Ruthless in a competitive struggle, destroying a rival without compunction, indifferent to social conditions that lead to failure and dire need.

From this derives a tolerance of waste; social as well as material. Waste in production and distribution, waste in government, waste in the conduct of men's lives. But likewise an undying optimism grounded on the assurance that no man can exhaust the possibilities of success.

From optimism generates an acceptance of change. The traditional American lives neither in the past nor in the present, but in the future. Even when he "points with pride" to his achievements; the business created, the city builded, the roads constructed, the thousand and one gadgets devised to ease the material side of life, he does so merely in order to suggest the outlines of a bigger and better tomorrow.

It is upon this assumption of desirable change that the civil rights of thought, of speech, of the press are grounded. Only when society settles down into grooves, or when weak old men and insecure young men become fearful of what tomorrow holds in store does the exercise of civil rights seem fraught with danger. A young democracy faces the future with confidence and prizes civil rights as the conscious instruments of orderly change.

All of this is but saying that democracy in the United States has typified until recently the spirit of youth. The atmosphere in which it grew and took shape has been that of a young country. And well might this be so since young people have dominated our population. For example, in 1850 there were 890 adults to each 1000 young people under 16 years of age, in contrast with some 2100 adults today for each 1000 under 16 years of age. In other words, we are now in process of becoming a population of middle-aged and old people.

A middle-aged population will wish to revise the attitudes toward life and toward people that characterized its childhood and youth. And so is it with our American philosophy of life. Out of adversity as well as prosperity, out of the soil of a country recently come of age there has evolved a second philosophy of American democracy that contrasts at many points with the one sketched above.

What are its essential elements?

III

It begins with a repudiation of *laissez faire* in economic life and the conception of the individual as an independent entity. Its advocates remind us that economic society is no longer composed of small owners who manage their own property but, on the contrary, that business and industry are dominated by large organizations of capital which are social in composition, if not in management. Concentration of economic power rather than individual ownership and control, characterize both the production and the marketing of products today.

For example, the Temporary National Economic Committee, dealing with the structure of Industry, records a study of 1807 manufactured products. It was found that four manufacturers produced 85 per cent or more of the output in the case of one-third of these products, 75 per cent or more in one-half, and 50 per cent or more in three-fourths of the 1807 products studied. Technological developments have placed a premium upon large-scale production with the requirements of huge aggregations of capital and an increasing refinement and specialization of knowledge and skill. Improved transportation and means of communication render the marketing and the distribution of goods and services at once a more feasible and an increasingly complicated and complex process. Free competition between individuals who could possess themselves of capital or stake off a claim in a public domain rich in soil, mineral, timber, or power easily generated the notion of rugged individualism. But the disappearance of the frontier and the development of large-scale production have resulted in a crude form of socialization of capital and services not as yet harmonized with democracy. Doubtless the unification of the two will require transformation in the forms of both. Obviously the capital now used in industry and business is social in its origin while remaining individual in its distribution and rewards. It represents an association of inventors as well as producers. Furthermore, success in conducting an enterprise today is more and more contingent upon factors operating outside a particular industry or business as well as beyond the responsibility of one individual's judgment. If natural rubber, for instance, ceases to be a profitable product on the market and rubber plantations deteriorate or revert to nature, this cannot be charged to the failure of management as such. The same may be said of any number of products that face replacement in the near future by the manufacture of synthetic substitutes. It means merely that science has become a new and profitable source of raw materials.

But science so applied is a cooperative enterprise. Increasingly scientific research is carried on in conjunction with others, and less and less as an individual undertaking. Consequently, and with convincing plausibility, many contend that since the products flowing from scientific research are social in origin they should be made social in their contributions. Following the single-taxers of some years back they hold that just as it is unfair for the accidental owner of property to reap the sole reward of the community's contribution to the value of a piece of land, so it is unjust for an individual or a corporation to secure the lion's share of profits deriving from scientific research.

At all events it seems clear that the new economic development, if it is to conserve and develop the democratic spirit, must employ and respond to a larger and more generous capital of human resources and motives than hitherto. We have learned that while men must have bread in order to live, they cannot live on bread alone. Democracy requires us to plan all phases of our life, economic, political, social, with reference to the psychological and spiritual needs of human beings.

This implies the revision of our traditional conceptions of the nature of the individual.

We are becoming increasingly aware today of the social constitution of the human personality. From the perspective of the present we can see that pioneer life placed a premium upon traits such as resourcefulness and initiative, independence and self-control, and endurance to such a degree that men overlooked their social origin. The loneliness and isolation of frontier existence, the remoteness of government and organized social institutions from the average person encouraged the notion of man's independence of man. Actually, however, the mobility of American life meant that the process of clearing land and opening up new communities was repeated from generation to generation. Son learned from father and daughter from mother; and the habits as well as the instruments and devices acquired in one place, and at one time, were used with appropriate modification to solve the problems of another. So, too, the isolation of families, but nevertheless the dependence on occasion of neighbor upon neighbor, gave rise to social habits and traits of character peculiar to these conditions. In other words, rugged individualism expressed at its best a way of living appropriate to the social and physical environment of the American frontier. The very qualities that enabled man to do without man testified to his indebtedness to others!

Certain it is that early notions of the individual and of his relations to society are under review today. Students of human nature no longer conceive of people as existing apart from society or as primarily reasoning beings. They point out that the concept of the rational man and of the relation of the individual to society underlying early individualism antedates scientific psychology. They insist that a study of the development of an individual reveals him at no time as insulated from a social medium. From the moment of conception his life is involved in the life of another. At birth he is taken care of by a mother or by a nurse and is thus early influenced by the adults' peculiar ways of behaving, feeling, and thinking. His first habits are established by them—habits of eating, ideas of cleanliness, notions of right relations with others. He is guarded and supervised and guided. Thus his first basic emotional attitudes are built into him. He sees and feels and interprets the world through the colored glasses of the human beings with whom he is living. Out of this social medium he creates his personality. Moreover he is first of all and primarily an emotional, feeling being; and it is emotionally that he establishes his fundamental attitudes toward life, depending upon the kind of people with whom he associates and the quality of relations which obtain between father and mother, parents and children, child and child within the family. These relationships stamp his fundamental attitudes as those of confidence and assurance, or fear, frustration, futility. They determine whether he shall be normally friendly or hostile toward others, frank and free, inhibited or timid. These early attitudes likewise ordain how he is to relate himself to others when he leaves home to "go on his own."

This concept of an organic individual is gaining credence today. According to it, reason, or the rational attitude, is not something that one possesses natively; it is the result of discipline, of growth, of the way in which each one copes with the circumstances of his life. Consequently it is supremely important for schools and homes to cooperate in building the fundamental emotional attitudes indispensable for growth into a rational being. It is likewise necessary for adults to equip the young person, by means of the life they live with him, to employ methods of reason. And it is supremely important, in these perilous days, for schools and homes to help young people to understand the fundamental assumptions and values of life that constitute the major premises of democratic intercourse; the assumptions and values which men can employ in solving democratically the specific problems of living.

But all of this has to be acquired. It is a gift of education, not of nature.

Now, just as the individual is more social in his constitution than we once thought, so, too, society is more personal in nature than we once believed. Sociologists, such as Robert Lynd, tell us that society or culture should be viewed "as living in and operating as the learned habits and impulses of persons." Our culture is thus the common, characteristic ways in which we think, feel, behave. Are you subjected to the pressures of society? What is this other than the way in which people around you and with whom you are emotionally identified and thus to whom you are sensitive, actually feel, think, and behave? You experience pressure because you are inclined to do as they do or as they will; in short, their purposes are really a part of you. You are in some respects one with them; the way in which they view the world and would have you act is of import to you.

This organic conception of man and his society bears directly upon the way in which we envisage relations between groups, whether these be within a nation or between nations. In either case it follows that man cannot live unto himself alone. Nor does the government consist of an entity distinct from the governed. It is rather an agency, or an association of agencies, devised by people to serve certain defined purposes.

To grasp this idea and to employ it constructively requires an abandonment of shibboleths such as National Sovereignty and Sacred Interests inherited from the long ago but restored to vigor by modern dictators. These thrive when government is thought of as the personal possession of an individual or a group embodying in itself sovereignty. Personal government can exercise a will and maintain a status of its own. Its interest and national honor exist as something separate and distinct from the welfare of its people. But democratic governments eliminate these vestiges of an older order since they grow out of and constitute vital relationships between individuals and peoples. Nor are they something above and beyond the instruments created with which to minister to the needs of men.

Need we add that this concept of the state, of society, and culture, carries a moral for relations between nations? As against rugged individualism on an international plane it holds that nations, as individuals, are interdependent. In the modern world of easy communication the interests of nations and of groups within nations interpenetrate. We can transform this interdependence into organized interrelationship under the ideal of mutuality in living. This point of view leads men to strive not for a League of Nations organized on the principle of self-determination, in which a collection of sovereign nations seek each to realize its selfish interests with a minimum of responsibility for common obligations. It envisages rather an international order genuinely organic in character in which cultural distinctions are harmonized with international law, and national sovereignty is replaced by a genuine international association of peoples.

IV

We thus observe two contrasting theories of democracy in this country with which a teacher, who is seriously concerned to use the school as an introduction to contemporary American society, must acquaint his students. They constitute the large outlines of two world views. The conflict in values thus involved explains controversies in community and state with respect to the creation and the maintenance of governmental services. Shall schools provide health and recreational services, free text books, school luncheons, an enriched curriculum; or shall they remain true to the essentials of an education? Shall the community provide public housing, health centers, low-priced medical care and hospital service; or shall it refuse to "pauperize" its inhabitants? Should the federal government intervene on behalf of youth along lines tentatively explored some years ago by the Civilian Conservation Corps and the National Youth Administration; or should it consider education of all types and for all ages strictly a state and local responsibility? Should our country follow in the path of Theodore Roosevelt armed with the big stick; or heed the example of Franklin Roosevelt and explore the possibilities of the Good Neighbor policy?

Each of these views, in its own way, respects the integrity of personality and the worth of the individual, but one would encourage the expression of worth and uniqueness with the minimum of intervention by others, and the second would use the agencies of society in order to foster the development of free personalities. Both rely upon free government, but the first conceives social instruments as at best friendly aliens, while the second envisages society and its institutions as "a set of learned instrumental ways of behaving with which human beings seek to realize their needs."

Teachers need not attempt to indoctrinate one interpretation of democracy as against the other in the classroom, but it is doubtful whether they can avoid deciding which they will use in organizing and carrying on the life of the school. We are living in days when the meaning of democracy must be clarified in the mind of each citizen and of each prospective citizen for whom it is to serve as a living faith. This clarification can come about only through the process of comparison and contrast not merely of democracy and fascism or communism, but of the rival philosophies of life that struggle for supremacy within the democracies themselves.

CHAPTER II

Are We Master or Servant in Our House?

WERE it possible to view the lives of nations as the lives of men we might contrast the plight of modern America with the plight of Job of old. Certainly as Job was favored by the Lord so our Republic has been favored; and as Job was subjected to trial so are we sorely tried. And we, like Job, search our hearts for an explanation of the evil that has befallen us.

The occasion of Job's ordeal was a day on which the sons of God presented themselves before the Lord. Satan, we are told, was one of them.

"And the Lord said unto Satan, 'Hast thou considered my servant Job, that there is none like him in the earth, a perfect and an upright man, one that feareth God and escheweth evil?' "

Satan answered the Lord in words which we might use to describe the state of our nation in the early years of the present century:

"Hast not thou made a hedge about him, and about his house, and about all that he hath on every side? Thou hast blessed the work of his hands, and his substance is increased in the land."

We must not press our analogy too far. At no time have conditions in America been ideal. Poverty, injustice, and maladjustments have dwelt with us. But, on the whole, we have prospered. An open country and the matchless resources of soil, mine and forest generated for a time a widespread well-being and an optimistic Amercian temperament.

Then came rapid changes. Transformations stole upon us like a thief in the night. Consequently we search confusedly for explanations and causes. In common with the natural tendency of men, we are easily convinced that evils result from sin. Grievously we suffer; therefore grievously must we have erred. As Eliphaz the Temanite said of Job, so say we of ourselves,

"Who ever perished, being innocent? Or where were the righteous cut off?"

With the conviction of sin comes a natural tendency to return to the faith of our fathers; to ways of life—more accurately, to ways of thinking about life, that were abandoned in the days of our prosperity and ease. It is not strange, then, to encounter in American society not merely reversions to orthodoxy in religion but reactionary tendencies in education and politics as well.

II

First of these atavistic tendencies is a lack of faith in man.

In religious circles this is marked by an abandonment of the "Social Gospel," a movement intended to offset the individualistic emphasis of early American religious thought. This trend was evident some years ago in all denominations, Protestant, Catholic, and Jewish alike. Particularly was it influential prior to the first World War. In contrast with the traditional injunction to render unto Caesar the things that are Caesar's, it stressed the importance of establishing the Kingdom of God on earth. It strove manfully to turn certain principles of Christianity toward the creation of a new social and economic order. The Social Gospel breathed confidence, perhaps an overconfidence in man and his possibilities; thus contrasting with the ancient, pessimistic notion of man and of nature. It recognized the influence of environment upon the quality of man's will. Tacitly, if not openly and frankly, it accepted the non-dependence of moral conduct upon religious belief, certainly upon theological belief. It fostered an indifference not merely in the laity but on the part of the clergy as well, to theology. Under this impulse the lines that had long divided religious denominations tended to disappear and, within religion itself, the spirit of secular concern for the conditions of a good life became a bond of union between churches and congregations, even though the nature of this Good Life was none too clearly defined.

Today all this is changed. Frequently the identical individuals who some years ago issued a clarion call for social reconstruction on behalf of the Kingdom of God on earth, characterize these efforts as evidence of inordinate "pride and egoism." They urge man to center upon his relation to God, since he can not save himself. Gone are the efforts to define God in terms of a quickened social consciousness. God is now pictured as a Being removed from the affairs of men, sanctioning, if not encouraging, a like complacency on the part of man with respect to the evils of the world. As Harrison Elliott has stated:

Liberal ministers and theologians have said that we have moved too far in the democratization of God and religion. What is needed is a recognition of man's sinfulness and inadequacy and of the power and transcendence of God. American religious liberals have criticized it as drastically as a Barth or a Brunner. It was a sentimental dream and did not take into account the hard facts of man's egoistic and sinful nature and his inability to do anything significant about his own affairs. . . . It has been the emphasis upon man's sin and guilt and upon his dependence upon the grace of God which has seemed to be predominant.[1]

A second tendency in American life is marked by a return to authoritarianism in morality and the pursuit of truth.

This is aided and abetted by our Puritan tradition which combined both democratic and absolutistic elements. For example, the Puritan stressed the importance of an education sufficient to enable each one to read and interpret the Bible

[1] *Frontiers of Democracy*, Vol. VI, May, 1940, p. 237. New York: Progressive Education Association. For a full discussion of this tendency in connection with the problem of religious education see Harrison Elliott, *Can Religious Education Be Religious?* New York: The Macmillan Company, 1940.

for himself. Negatively this was intended as a device for evading that "old deluder Satan" who seeks to keep people in ignorance of the Scriptures. Positively it insured each individual the opportunity to discover, on his own responsibility, the true way of salvation. (Certainly a crucial test of democracy, since the individual's prospects for eternal bliss or damnation hung upon the correctness of his interpretation!)

But the true way of salvation was not an individual creation. It existed ready-made. The definition of right and wrong, down to the minutest detail of correct thought and action, was contained within the Bible. Knowledge and truth thus existed independently of man. Accordingly, the wise man disciplined his mind and will alike to the injunctions of the Lord as set forth in the somewhat ambiguous words of the Scripture.

In a recent volume entitled, *The Destiny of Western Man*, W. T. Stace describes the attempt of contemporary thinkers to rescue moral theory from this trend of thought which he ascribes to our Palestinian inheritance. This influence, he states, has long permeated the European mind. It roots ethical principles in the commands of God, commands that are imposed upon a nature essentially alien to them, since man is "naturally" disposed toward evil.

Stace would replace this authoritarian conception of morality with an immanent theory, derived in large measure from Plato and the Greeks.

Stace points out that the Greek in his search for the right way of living, relied upon his own resources. He was convinced that religious doctrine constitutes an uncertain foundation upon which to ground morality. Indeed his problem consisted precisely in the opposite approach, since he was impelled to rescue moral principles from the corrupting influences of religion. His gods defied all standards of decency as well as of morality. They stole, they lied, they cheated, they committed adultery. Consequently, when the mortal Greek sought to purify morality and to justify right behavior, he turned not to religion but to the constitution of human nature itself.

It thus did not occur to Plato that human impulses are a species of original sin. As he saw it, goodness and badness follow from the use to which impulses are put, not from their nature. The appetites of hunger and sex, for example, are good in themselves. Only when carried to excess or misdirected do they become gluttony and adultery. To realize the good life, one must learn to bring about the proper functioning of his nature. Plato conceived this to be threefold: reason, spirit, appetite. In the supremacy of reason man finds his happiness since reason gives balance to appetite and spirit.

Now, what interests us in this is not merely the fact that Plato grounds morality in reason; but that reason is viewed as a normal constituent of man's nature. Morality is thus analogous to good health; it is the happy realization of a proper functioning of our nature.

Unfortunately it was also Plato who undermined this naturalistic conception of morality. In his well-known allegory of the captives chained with their backs to the opening of a cave so that they can see only shadows upon the wall, he suggests that we, as they, fall into the error of identifying reflections from reality with reality itself.

In Aristotle and his successors the effects of nostalgia become more manifest. Aristotle likens the sojourn of the soul within the body to an illness, and life without the body to the normal state of the soul. For Aristotle, also, the highest function of the soul is thinking, while God is envisaged as pure, self-sustained thinking. On the other hand, matter without thought is formless. What we call species, classes of things, types of action, forms of life, derive from the fact that creative thought has, so to speak, carved them out of a formless non-being.

Observe what has happened. We began with a rough and ready distinction between matter and form, body and mind, action and principle of action. This is now transformed into a *distinction of kind;* the one higher than the other by nature and thus superior. Moreover, a common-sense conception of the place of reason in the direction of men's lives, the normal function of weighing and appraising behavior, the attempt to give balance and perspective to conduct, that is, reasoning as an *operation,* is thought of as a Faculty of Reason, a principle subsisting apart from time and space, capable of penetrating into human experience, determining the nature of right and wrong and giving validity and sanctity to one line of conduct as against another. Reason, by means of a sleight-of-hand performance on the part of the philosophers, acquires a capital letter and an authoritarian status that reflects suspiciously the differences in social and economic and political status between the higher and the lower classes in the society giving birth to this philosophy!

It is impossible to trace the steps by means of which the early Christian God of decidedly anthropomorphic characteristics, of love and kindness, anger and jealousy, became identified with the conception of an absolute reason; or the manner in which the idea of habitual obedience, so rigorously exacted by Jehovah, likewise came to apply to the logical relationships obtaining between a general principle and the applications of this principle to concrete situations. Were we to do so, we should observe the evolution of a religion of duty, and the concept of right for Right's sake.

Probably the most impressive and influential formulation of this principle finds expression in the German philosopher Kant. Kant distinguishes rigidly between two types of moral acts: one, obedience to a Conditional Ought, and one to an Unconditional.

The response to a conditional ought is of a practical nature. It relates means to foreseen ends. It is action that "depends" on some end we wish to realize, or on circumstance. For example, we may say, "I ought to save money in order not to burden my children in my old age." Or, "I ought to

give my children the advantages of a good education in order
to discharge my responsibilities as a parent." Such conditional
oughts relate a proposed line of behavior to circumstances of
a foreseeable character. The relations of means to ends are
scrutinized and circumstances enter to weight decisions. Because the ought is related thus to the practical, Kant considers it not quite moral.

The Unconditional Ought is of a different nature. It derives from *Pure Reason* and is totally unrelated to consequences. It is right for Right's sake. The agreement of a con-
templated line of action with the dictates of Pure Reason
follows from a decision to obey these dictates irrespective
of human disposition or inclination or desire or foreseen consequences. Indeed a consideration of the practical implications or the possible consequences to us of the principle is
thought to lead us astray. The eye, in a pure, moral act, must
contemplate Duty and Right only, without reference to
human or mundane interests.

Does this seem abstract and remote, even far fetched? Perhaps. But acquiescence in this theory of moraltiy explains in
part the submission of a people to a totalitarian government.
And, at least in diluted form, all of us are influenced by the
doctrine of principle for principle's sake.

Suppose, for example, that a people can be induced to believe the injunctions of the Unconditional Ought are identical with the will of the men who control the State; as is true
of Germany and Japan. What follows? No claims that normally bind husband and wife, child and parent, no consideration of gentle relations between people can stand in the way
of duty! And thus do men suddenly discover to their horror,
that what began as a noble resolve to subordinate caprice to
reason, ends with the sacrifice of humane values upon the
altar of a ruthless and unadulterated Power!

Obviously Germany and Japan have no monopoly on the
philosophy of absolutism. We point to these nations merely
to illustrate the effects upon a people when moral ideas be-

come as putty in the hands of an unquestioned authority.

No, Germany and Japan are not alone in their allegiance to this method of thinking or the philosophy that gave birth to it. In recent years we have had a resurgence of absolutism in American education, philosophy, and social science.

For example, recent attempts of Robert M. Hutchins, Mortimer Adler, Stringfellow Barr and others to reform American education are represented at times in terms not unlike the one described. These men berate American educators for their attempt to adapt schools to the needs of young people in a rapidly changing world. "The notion of educating a man to live in any particular time or place, to adjust him to any particular environment, is therefore foreign to a true conception of experience," exclaims President Hutchins. "Education implies teaching. Teaching implies knowledge. Knowledge is truth. The truth is everywhere the same. Hence education should be everywhere the same."[2]

Accordingly Hutchins scorns education through first-hand experience and urges us to return to the writings of the masters. From these may be derived the unchanging principles of knowledge that alone give direction to the particulars of living.

So, too, we find Mortimer Adler constructing a philosophical foundation for the return of religious and philosophical absolutism not only in education but also in the affairs of the state; a philosophical grounding of what he insists is democracy, although others will detect a closer resemblance to authoritarianism. Thus, in a paper entitled "God and the Professors,"[3] read at the Conference on Science, Philosophy, and Religion in Relation to the Democratic Way of Life, in 1941, Mortimer Adler concludes that the positivism of the professors in our colleges today "is the central corruption of

[2] *The Higher Education in America,* p. 66. New Haven: Yale University Press, 1936.

[3] *In Science, Philosophy and Religion, First Symposium,* p. 128. Published by Conference on Science, Philosophy, and Religion in Relation to the Democratic Way of Life, Inc.

modern culture." "Democracy," he holds, "has much more to fear from the mentality of its teachers than from the nihilism of Hitler." When we inquire more closely into the nature of this dangerous positivism, we discover it consists in a failure to admit the superiority of philosophy and metaphysics over science as well as the claim of religion to dominate our culture. "Religion," he insists, "is either the supreme Human discipline, because it is God's discipline of man, and as such dominates our culture, or it has no place at all. The mere toleration of religion which implies indifference to or denial of its claims, produces a secularized culture as much as militant atheism or Nazi nihilism."[4]

In his book entitled *The Crisis of Our Age*,[5] P. A. Sorokin of Harvard University adds the weight of a social scientist to this absolutistic trend. According to Sorokin, it is the dominance of our sensate culture, our pre-occupation with things of the sense, which explains the crisis of our times. "In our zeal to serve mammon," he exclaims, "we have forgotten God."

No one will deny that material values have tended to dominate American life. Nor is this surprising when we reflect that America has attracted for some three centuries the hungry and the destitute from all parts of the earth; people who sought to find here the material basis for a better life. Should we not expect them, for a time, to over-value the material means of their salvation?

Not Sorokin. As he sees it, this in no way explains our difficulties. He believes we are living in the final days of a fading culture. A careful reading of history, he holds, reveals three main forms of culture: the ideational, the sensate, and (as a blending of the two) the idealistic. The history of civilization merely records the passage of peoples through these cultural forms. The dominant theme in an ideational culture is religious and other-worldly; as, for example, in

[4] *Ibid.*, p. 131.
[5] New York: E. P. Dutton & Co., Inc., 1941.

medieval life, where science, philosophy, religion, art, economic, political, and social life—all gave exclusive expression to and were dominated by the principle of "a supersensory and superrational God."

Contrasted with the supersensory and superrational characteristics of the ideational culture is the sensory. In this a superrational and supersensory God is denied by the dominant forces of the time. These forces ascribe reality and value only to what men can see, hear, smell, touch or otherwise perceive through the senses. Sorokin contents that this tendency has characterized a dominant motif in the past four centuries. Between these two periods appears the most adequate form of culture. It is idealistic in its mixture of ideational and sensory elements, blending the principles of a supersensory and superrational order with the sensory into a unity under the "infinite manifold, God." Sorokin considers that the civilization of Europe in the thirteenth and fourteenth centuries and of Greece in the fourth and fifth centuries exemplify "this synthesizing major premise."

This analysis foreshadows a ringing out of the period in which we live. Nor is there anything we can do except perhaps to cooperate with the inevitable movement of history. The sensory culture, enveloping us, will continue to disintegrate. Consequently, we should expect increasing chaos and confusion in our systems of values as well as in our mental and moral lives. Wars will continue, and other evils that flow inevitably from our materialistic and relativistic ethics and philosophy will flourish.

To be sure there is comfort in the conviction that all of this is but one phase in the grand movement of history; that sensory reality and value are but one of the aspects of the infinitely richer true reality and value; that those have a supersensory aspect of which we get a glimpse through our reason and through charismatic grace or intuition in its sublime forms; that this supersensory side is the supreme aspect of the value-reality, and as such it is absolute; that the same is true in regard to the reality and value of man and of the sublimest flowers of his culture.[6]

The moral of this diagnosis is to observe that science, religion, philosophy, ethics and art should serve but one purpose: "the unfolding of the Absolute in the relative, empirical world, to the greater nobility of man and the greater glory of God."[7] Once we succeed in effecting this transformation in our mentality there will follow corresponding changes in social relationships and forms of social organization with "purer and more godly familistic relationships."[8] Precisely what "familistic relationships" imply, however, is a technical detail Sorokin leaves unexplained! But may not the suspicious and unregenerate inquire, why this emphasis upon a familistic relationship unless there be as well a *pater familias?*

Authoritarianism assumes different forms: philosophical, religious, political. In each instance the source and the ultimate criterion of the right varies. For one the final source of values is a metaphysical reality altogether freed of anthropomorphic characteristics; for another it is the command of a personal and a jealous God; for still a third a Common Will embodied in an earthly State. In each case the supreme arbiter of John Doe's fate is in no way controlled by or contingent upon John Doe. The crucial decisions of his life, the values to which he must give the last full measure of devotion are formulated independently of him. His function is to do or to die, not to reason why.

Let us keep in mind that the question at issue for the moment is not the truth or the falsity or, for that matter, the necessity of a belief in a supernatural or a transcendental reality. It is rather the part that a free man can play in regulating his own fate, with or without a friend behind phenomena. Whether he shall consider himself a necessary par-

[6] *Ibid.,* p. 316.
[7] *Ibid.,* p. 318.
[8] *Ibid.,* p. 320.

ticipant, a deciding factor, at least a co-creator of good and evil, or merely a straw in the cosmic wind.

Undoubtedly it is a source of comfort for people, who are impelled so to do, to believe in a power, not ourselves, that makes for righteousness. It affords them comfort and an assurance they might not otherwise possess. So, too, there is security in the conviction that we do not live unto ourselves alone. Just as, educators have learned, no one type of teacher-pupil relationship will meet the varying needs of all children (some requiring careful control and guidance and others greater freedom to go it alone, as a means in each case of acquiring ultimately the ability for self-direction and independent action) so do adults differ in their spiritual demands upon the universe. These demands reflect inner needs. They derive, perhaps, from the nature of emotional development in childhood, as much as from the quality of the philosophic and religious inquiry of later years.

These needs are to be respected. But again, just as a wise teacher approves of a control and a discipline that fosters strength of will and, ultimately, an ability on the part of the child to decide independently how he shall govern his actions, so should we appraise the worth of the moral and ethical principles men employ accordingly as they encourage or discourage moral independence.

Let us examine the effects of authoritarianism from this point of view. How does it equip men to play the part of mature adults in a democratic society?

III

Obviously it tends to undermine the status of the common man. The moment he surrenders to priest or king, Fuehrer or philosopher, the right to interpret or to define for him the values he holds supreme and to which he dedicates the last full measure of his devotion, the way of democracy becomes hard.

This is not to uphold for a moment the ways in which

men have used their freedom in our partial democracies. Like the privileged classes they, too, have sinned grievously in their prosperity. It is often true, as Sorokin charges, that people have exaggerated the importance of material comforts, goods and services. They have succumbed to sensate values and have frequently been soft and selfish.

Who can defend, for example, the manner in which groups that have struggled through blood and sweat and tears to win the rights and privileges and enjoyments of free men deny to others the opportunity to attain similar status? And yet, is this not precisely what happens when colored workers and other minority groups are denied equal treatment by American labor? Or who can justify the rules determining the distribution of rewards in business and industry under our *laissez faire* policy? Rewards that sanction conspicuous waste on the part of a few and conditions of poverty and under-nourishment of soul and body for the many?

But, let it be observed, we do condemn these practices! And thus do we bear witness to the principles of equality and fraternity that free men envision. This insures an ultimate revision of practice. These principles promise balance and proportion in the good things of life, not merely as between groups but in the ordering of each man's personal existence. Extravagance and waste and injustice are recognized for what they are, evidences of immaturity and crudity in adults as well as children that we have reason to believe education can cure.

At all events the remedy is not to deny the importance of material goods as such but rather to improve the quality of their use at the same time we busy ourselves to make them more widely available.

The absolutist adopts a different solution. He would have the masses throw out the baby of material goods with the bath. Lest he acknowledge the claims of material advantages and the pleasures of the flesh he condemns sensate values altogether. Accordingly he has little to say of ways in which tastes can be refined or order and quality imposed upon the products of a technological civilization. On the contrary, he creates categories of classification between goods and values that are arbitrary if not unreal. He seeks to induce men to put behind them the appeal of sensate values and to dedicate their lives instead to Duty or Principle. But the full implication of these claims are not foreseen or comprehended by those who are thus asked to obey, since they have not participated in defining the content of Duty and Principle.

The absolutist is thus in danger of subjecting himself and others to the errors of the people of Germany, where, as Max Otto has said, Kant's noble theory turned out to be "a book of checks, made out to the bearer on demand, signed by the blind sense of duty, and good for whatever amount the holder may have the will to write in, and the power to collect."[9]

Nor do we lack evidence of what can happen here when people are frustrated over long periods of time or are deprived of the means whereby they can assure themselves of good food, comfortable and attractive clothing, housing adequate for the refinements of living, play and recreation, and a satisfying social status. It is these malformed and distorted personalities who become easy fodder for the fascist-minded, or of demagogues who persuade them readily to barter away their claim to "empty" democratic values, in return for promises of a land of plenty in which they will occupy an assured status of racial and religious superiority and economic abundance.

A second danger in the tendencies described, follows from the effort to emasculate human nature; to divide it into parts, one higher and the other lower, one body and the other soul, one the life of reason and the other of impulse and emotion. The lines of division and the methods of classification differ as between schools of thought, but all agree in denying to man some aspect of his nature that is uniquely and essentially

[9] *Things and Ideals*, p. 74. New York: Henry Holt & Co., 1924.

his. Ways of functioning that seem qualitatively different under varying conditions are interpreted as divisions of substance and reality—such as the natural man of emotion and impulse, mostly evil, and a spiritual nature that responds to laws and principles not acclimated to the natural order.

Actually, of course, man is an emotional, social and rational being capable of responding in varied ways. He can hate, but he can also love with unbelievable self-forgetfulness. He can be selfish and cruel, generous and tender; self-abasing and non-competitive; self-seeking and aggressive; rational and irrational. Which of these qualities he manifests at any one moment depends upon training and insight and the circumstances and conditions prevailing at the time. And which of these will constitute permanent attitudes and dispositions varies with experience and education.

Of importance also is the conviction men hold regarding the nature of human nature itself. Once we convince man that he is by nature an animal, in the sense that he possesses only the derogatory qualities of animals, or that desirable characteristics such as unselfishness, generosity, cooperation, rational behavior are foreign to him, we weaken his resources at their source.

As evidence of this fact we may observe the history of the Social Gospel movement, to which we referred earlier. This movement began as a positive factor on behalf of social change. As against an earlier preoccupation with individual salvation from sin the Social Gospel movement was concerned to bring about a new social order on earth. In recent years, however, a reversion to the old position is discernible. And, ironically, as Harrison Elliott states, the leaders in the former movement now characterize their earlier efforts as evidences of

man's sinful presumption and egotism in thinking he could do anything significant about human affairs. God is the ruler of this universe. It is his will which dominates the universe and the world. The human problem, therefore, is to make one's peace with this divine ruler. There is no hope of bringing God's reign in human affairs. Human effort is sinful and under God's condemnation.[10]

Unfortunately, in their optimistic days these theologians did not abandon the historical division of man's nature into two parts. They still viewed man as born in sin. Consequently when evil days fell upon them they abandoned hope and found it easier to believe that man is doomed to his sinful state than to cope courageously with the enemy at the gates.

IV

Retreat is one method of meeting a crisis. Still another is to surrender to the enemy. The latter is characteristically the way of the cynic, the materialist and the behaviorist. When this group confronts the traditional division of man's nature into higher and lower—mind and body, spirit and matter—in which the higher is said to comprise the nobler psychological and moral qualities and the lower the mechanical and more beastlike characteristics, it denies the existence of the spiritual and ascribes reality only to matter and motion. This was the method of Hobbes and it is substantially the method of present-day behaviorists. Accordingly idealistic, spiritual, non-selfish traits assume an unreal and illusory form. Thinking is reduced to muscle movement; reason is explained as nothing more than a complicated pattern of habits; ideals are composites of specific reactions to given situations; and education becomes an instrument by means of which one generation "conditions" another with the habits and skills it wishes to perpetuate. Moral behavior is evidence of habits thus instilled.

An illustration of this cynical attitude is found in the "scientific" education of some years ago. This attained influence and prominence in the years following the first World War. In retrospect it appears as one result of the disillusionment of the period, but it was also a logical outgrowth of the mechan-

[10] *Op. cit.,* p. 236.

ical and behaviorist psychology then prevalent. This school conceived of all learning as habit formation and habit as the establishment of "bonds" between reaction systems and stimulating situations. The teaching of a subject such as arithmetic became merely a matter of forming "bonds in the nervous system between stimuli and responses," and the introduction of young people to the life of a good citizen a problem of identifying the desirable "traits" of a citizen, analyzing these into their simplest components of behavior, and devising effective situations in school designed to incorporate them in the nervous systems of the young.

The task of education, as the scientists in education saw it, is both more complicated and far simpler than commonly conceived. More complicated in that each idea and each action of an ideal adult must be acquired, under ideal conditions, by each child and cannot be left to chance or originality; more simple, in that each detail of growing up is subject, potentially, to detailed control and direction. Everything essential in life can be taught, in direct proportion to the possession of an appropriate I.Q.!

This procedure carried its moral for education in a democracy. As Ross Finnery emphasized in *A Sociological Philosophy of Education,*[11] written under the inspiration of this period, the common notion that every citizen in a democracy should be urged to think for himself is fallacious. He points to the results of intelligence tests which confirm the fact that the average citizen possesses a very low intelligence indeed. Accordingly, he writes,

> The safety of democracy is not to be sought, therefore, in the intellectual independence of the duller masses but in their intellectual dependence. Not in what they think, but in what they think they think.

And again,

> And it is principally through the schools that this new coinage of the collective intellect should be paid into general circulation.

[11] P. 390. New York: The Macmillan Company, 1929.

It is not enough that we teach children to think, we must actually force-feed them with the concentrated results of expert thinking. To this end there is immense occasion for memoriter training and sheer drill. Ours are the schools of a democracy, which *all* the children attend. At least half of them never had an original idea of any general nature, and never will. But they must behave as if they had *sound* ideas. Whether those ideas are original or not, matters not in the least. It is better to be right than to be original. . . . Instead of trying to teach dullards to think for themselves, the intellectual leaders must think for them, and drill the results, memoriter, into their synapses. For the dullards it is that or nothing.

The conclusion is obvious. A clear road ahead for the man of power or the group that can successfully gain control of the schools and use them to teach young people what they should know and do!

v

Does it not appear that the absolutist and the behaviorist alike are on dangerous ground? Do they not refuse to recognize in human beings the full promise of their natures? The behaviorist envisages man only as a complicated mechanism and, consequently, education degenerates into high grade animal training. The absolutist, on the other hand, bifurcates human nature. One part is the natural man, basically antisocial and prone to yield to the world of the flesh and the devil. The other is a rational or a spiritual nature, social in its leanings, but essentially alien to this world.

Neither description corresponds with recent investigations in psychology and anthropology. These studies reveal man neither as a thing of parts, something given once and for all in advance of experience, nor a being preordained for good or evil. They indicate rather that people throughout the world are extremely varied and flexible in their possibilities.

From anthropological and psychological research it is established that no one character trait is native or foreign as such to human beings. Character, rather, emerges out of the interplay of the individual with his social and physical environment. Personalities grow out of interrelationships with people and take form from the quality of these relationships. Accordingly, there is no scientific evidence for believing that either altruistic or selfish, lovely or unlovely impulses constitute the "normal" or "natural" constituents of behavior. They are at best possibilities that time and circumstance, in short, experience makes actual. Within each of us, moreover, are potentialities in excess of any possible realization. And the moral problem for each of us is how he can use to best advantage the capital in hand; how he can give organization and expression to the type of personality he most wishes to become; how he can create or control the conditions, physical and material as well as social, that will reinforce and nourish his deepest hopes and noblest aspirations.

The idea that morality cannot be defined as an ideal system of behavior apart from human beings and the particulars of living, that it is rather a creative process in which each individual is of necessity the architect of his own fortunes, is profoundly significant for democracy. It presupposes a society of free men. But a society of free men, to endure, must be conscious of its fundamental assumptions of living and succeed in translating its faith into action. Accordingly we turn to an affirmation of a free man's faith.

CHAPTER III

A Free Man's Faith

A NEWS dispatch from a remote point in the Pacific now used as a mobilizing center for American troops contrasts the general bearing and attitude of the expeditionary forces in the present war with those of 1917. According to this correspondent the boys of today are on the whole a quieter and more modest group than were those of 1917. They are less given to boasting and demonstration but no less dedicated to the task confronting them. They are more mature and more intelligently aware of the issues for which they are preparing to lay down their lives. They have learned in school that war is wasteful and a species of group insanity; but since they can discover no alternative to war as a means for checkmating the designs of the totalitarian nations, they are resolved to see it through even to the bitter end.

In this conviction and in this mood they are at one with the vast majority of the folks back home. As a nation we have taken up arms to safeguard the principles of democratic living in full realization that war is a most dangerous instrument to employ, fraught always with the possibilities of defeating the ends for which it is used.

This resignation of spirit derives from the obvious failure in the last World War to give body and substance to the ideals for which men died. Men fought a war "to end war"; a war to insure the self-determination of small nations as well as large; a war to make the world safe for democracy. Nevertheless within a few short years of the peace they dictated, they saw each one of these objectives transformed into its opposite. Small wonder, then, that all view anxiously the nature of the post-war world. Will the peace once more turn sour? Or is there the intelligence and the will this time to induce men literally to beat their swords into plowshares and their spears into pruning hooks?

There is some basis for believing that they will. From the failures of the past and, positively, from the science of both group and individual behavior the primary conditions of social health are now generally known. It remains for us to give them body. As against a purely punitive peace we must find the means of insuring a sense of security to all; a security that encourages men to view their futures in the spirit of adventure. Secondly, men must be guaranteed an endurable status, one that promotes confidence in their talents and possibilities. And, finally, we know that men should not feel alone in the world. Hence the privilege of belonging to some community, of living within the lives of others, must not be gainsaid.

How these essentials of peace are to be provided is more than an economic, a political, a social, or a psychological problem. No one of these means can be employed in isolation. Indeed the effective exercise of freedom and opportunity in any one area holds forth prospects of success only when envisaged as one aspect of a larger whole, of a philosophy of life.

It is thus our philosophy of life that will decide ultimately whether the peace we hope to win will endure. Should we revert, as we did following the last war, to a philosophy of individualism inherited in part from our pioneer days, in part from the concepts natural to the rugged conditions of the early stages of our industrial development, we shall fail a second time. Should we, however, seek to apply in our international associations the same principles of interrelationships we have recently found fruitful within our own borders, we can contemplate the future with sober optimism.

II

What is it we have learned in recent years that may be applied to a new world order?

Nothing less than the fact that we live in an interdependent world. Man cannot dwell in lonely isolation, even though he may will to do so. The doctrine of *laissez faire* in human relations, characteristic of our early individualism, cannot operate without injury in an interrelated society, either of individuals or nations.

This conclusion derives, as we observed in Chapter I, both from modern ways of living and from research and investigation into the nature of personality development. From these sources as well as from the long struggle through the ages to heighten the stature of man certain essential principles or assumptions of living have become evident, and upon these the free man may ground his faith.

To begin with, the free man has faith in the untapped resources of human personality. If we take the developmental approach not merely toward children, but toward adults as well, and utilize the facts that have emerged from studies in anthropology and sociology, from mental hygiene, child guidance clinics and psychiatric institutes, we have cause to believe that it is possible to organize ways of life in the home, in the school and in the community which will foster the growth of free personalities. Moreover, if we will but adapt this same knowledge to our treatment of backward peoples and to our future dealings with what James Marshall has termed "wayward nations,"[1] there is hope for building a more secure international society than in the past.

This faith in the educability of people, an expectation that under favorable circumstances and with intelligent and considerate treatment unforeseen possibilities will blossom forth

[1] See in this connection the suggestive chapter under this title in James Marshall's *The Freedom to Be Free*. New York: John Day, 1943.

from human beings, sustains the primary ethical principle of democracy; the dynamic conception of the worth of the individual, an attribution of respect and reverence for the integrity and the uniqueness of personality. A democracy anticipates that people will differ and it seeks in varied ways to use these differences for the enrichment of the common life.

This conception of worth has evolved out of age-long conflicts in religious, political, economic and social relationships. As an integral part of this process has come too a transformation in our ideas of how worth is to receive recognition. We have, for example, traveled far from the first naive conception that freedom and worth will attain reality by the simple act of removing obstructions. We now see that positive provision for growth must be made. We are convinced that personality is most truly seen not as an inner, individual affair, but as the product of interrelationships; that its quality is determined by conditions working upon it, as well as from the inmost urgings of the soul.

The early negative conception gave assurance to the optimism which permeated American life prior to the Civil War. It gave hope to the Perfectionist Movement, and oversimplified the task of social reformers who supported movements such as the abolition of slavery and prohibition. Even Emerson and his fellow Transcendentalists shared this easy notion of reform and regeneration. Thus in his essay on "Man The Reformer" Emerson writes:

"The power, which is at once spring and regulator in all efforts at reform, is the conviction that there is an infinite worthiness in man which will appear at the call of worth, and all particular reforms are the removing of some impediment."

This is a long way, of course, from the conception of the individual held by philosophers such as John Dewey, Felix Adler and the organismic school of educational psychology, which is today influencing so directly practice in modern schools. The earlier idea permits the individual to develop his powers if he can, and to realize his interests and his concerns with a clear conscience up to the point where so doing interferes with others. The later tests the value of these interests and concerns as well by means of their positive influence upon the lives of others. The earlier idea conceived society's duty as ended when impediments and shackles to freedom were removed. The second requires of society that it provide positive instruments to encourage and cultivate the unique qualities of the individual, and evaluates these qualities, at least in part, by the way they minister to the well-being of others.

Needless to say this faith contrasts with the time-honored theological conception of human beings as essentially evil and as born in sin, and it rejects modern variations upon the ancient theme of man's impotence and the ultimate futility of his endeavors to improve his lot. On the contrary, it holds that the rise of human beings from an original animal state, through barbarism, to the highest levels of civilization is prophetic of progress still ahead. Not by man's failures and regressions so much as by the highest and the best of his occcasional achievements do we know him.

On the other hand, confidence in people need cause us to labor under no illusions as to the nature of human progress. In no way does it imply that human advance is an automatic process or comes about as salvation by magic. It requires rather that we pin our faith on work; on work that painfully increases knowledge and skill; on the slow application of this knowledge and skill to the transformation of material conditions and changes in the manner of people's lives; and, in consequence, in the quality of their thinking, feeling and acting toward one another. In short, it sustains the doctrine that it is only by the sweat of the brow that men can learn to temper and refine their nature.

This confidence and reliance upon knowledge as a means of improvement causes us also to correlate progress with the improvement of education. That is, education broadly conceived.

Take, for example, family life. We can readily see that the tone and the character of good family life (apart from its material foundations) is primarily a matter of relations between personalities. Of a sensitiveness on the part of parents to the unique needs and characteristics of their children; of cordial and free and understanding relations between man and wife; of the ability of each member to enter sympathetically and appreciatively into the lives of other members and to regulate his behavior with a tender concern for what is thus revealed.

Now if we inquire how this type of family life can be realized more generally than at present, the answer is: by means of education. By putting into practice what is already known regarding the conditions of healthy personality development. Studies in mental hygiene, the practical work of child guidance clinics and family consultation bureaus have made available for our use the essential data and the tested procedures men need in order to enrich family life. What is lacking still is the dissemination and the use of this knowledge.

In later chapters we shall inquire more specifically what this education implies for the school. For the present we have in mind an education that utilizes science to foster free personalities in the sense of socially responsive personalities. Negatively this contrasts with much of the emphasis in many so-called progressive schools of recent years; schools which have been child-centered in the sense of involving the sacrifice of teachers and adults on the naive assumption that the selflessness of the adult would transfer by some magic to the child; schools which failed to observe that the child's interests are really social in origin and develop healthily only when they have what are to the child obvious social applications. Positively it means an education that is concerned with the all-round needs of children and adults.

This point of view also differs from the cult of hardness and discipline which many believe the war requires us to develop in our children. An externally imposed discipline fosters either a spineless docility or an indifference to others or both. Free, healthy personalities, in contrast, are sensitively constituted personalities, capable of entering sympathetically and imaginatively into the lives of their fellows and of responding generously to concerns other than their own. This requires discipline, but it is a discipline of a new order. It is moral discipline. Moral, because it directs the individual along lines of action with which he has freely identified himself. There is great need for self-imposed discipline in a democracy. A democracy dedicated to the pursuits of peace requires much less a discipline of passive obedience to another's command.

Good schools are essential for the development of personalities competent to function in a free society. But good schools alone will not insure that each young person will enter fruitfully into his inheritance. Schools, in other words, are not adequate unto themselves. The necessity that there be consistency and consecutiveness of influence in children's lives requires an intimate cooperation between school and home. Once the school envisages character education as a first responsibility it cannot ignore the home nor the opportunities of adult education. Thus do we conceive the school as reaching into the home, and conversely, the concerns of the home broadening the purposes and the work of the school.

Nor can we stop when intimate interrelationships of school and home are realized. The larger community also requires consideration. Children of minority groups carry with them into the school the evil effects of their out-of-school environment. They manifest feelings of inferiority and hostility that flow from injustices inflicted upon their families, or they bear witness in anti-social behavior to the disastrous consequences of social and economic disadvantage. This, too, constitutes an educational as well as a social and economic challenge.

The free man thus dedicates himself to the task of organizing ways of living which promote the healthy development of personalities. Moreover, he believes that this is peculiarly the function of government. He arrives at a principle of mutuality in the relationships of the individual and society. He believes the true relation between the individual and the group is one in which the group exists for the purpose of developing what is distinctive in the individual, and the individual develops his distinctiveness at its best only when in so doing he contributes to the welfare and similar development of others.[2]

This suggests a second article in the free man's faith.

If we conceive of society as the organized and habitual ways in which a people think, feel, and behave in response to conditions impinging upon them, then we have cause to believe that human ingenuity can transform both man and the conditions under which he lives. In other words, it is possible for us to envisage a society in which young and old can live healthily; a society from which depressed areas are removed and slums have disappeared; and in which young people have equal educational opportunities. We believe this can be brought about through man's efforts, and needs must be brought about because insight into the way in which personalities develop indicates that out of retarded living conditions come enemies, necessarily, of organized society; that there are environments which yield diseased personalities just as there are conditions which constitute diseased health areas.

A condition of our entering into this fuller life would seem to be a conscious acceptance of the principle that we live most truly when our lives are in tune with others and

[2] Felix Adler, *The Reconstruction of the Spiritual Ideal.* New York: D. Appleton and Co., 1924.

lasting satisfactions are envisaged as necessary components in the well-being of our fellows.

This principle runs counter to an atomistic conception of human nature of long standing. For centuries western man has sought the emancipation of the individual. But in seeking to root firmly the dignity of man in noble self-sufficiency he has tended often to nullify his spiritual union with his fellows. In ethics as well as in psychology and economics the individual has commonly been pictured as an isolated soul and only secondarily as a member of a social group. Protestantism with its emphasis upon personal salvation has reinforced this tendency and thus undermined the organic unity of human beings. Even modern psychology has started from the major premise that children are originally endowed with anti-social tendencies, instinctive ego drives, that involve them of necessity in conflict and hostility with their fellows.

Fortunately, today, these excesses in theory are undergoing correction and the conceptual foundations for an interdependent world are being laid. Psychologists, for example, now recognize the social constitution of the child. They observe that only gradually does a newborn child attain selfhood; a conscious independence of the adults who minister unto him. By the time he becomes an individual in his own right, he has absorbed many of the habits and attitudes, the characteristic emotions, the ways of feeling and of thinking of the group in which he has lived and moved and had his being. Just as a plant or the human body is a unique reconstruction of the physical elements and the chemical processes that minister to it, so is the human personality an individualized expression of the social influences that have pervaded it in the course of its existence.

Each of us is thus both one with his fellows and essentially distinct from them. Moreover, individual health as well as social well-being seems conditioned upon maintaining a delicate balance between this unity and difference. Isolate the individual from emotional identity with his fellows and he either withers and dies or grows into ugly proportions. Permit the social group to erase the distinctive qualities of individuals, and society too becomes either a monster or degenerates into dull uniformity.

In stressing that man does not live unto himself alone, we reject both rugged individualism and totalitarianism. Indeed, it is to be observed that the one is but an extreme reaction to the other. Nor can either long endure without injury alike to individual and social health.

Today it is the evils of individualism that beset life within the democracies. So serious are these evils that they threaten our national security as well as the intimate concerns of personal living.

Take, for example, the economic field. As indicated earlier, manufacture and trade were once severely handicapped by self-seeking restrictions imposed by upper-class governing groups. Consequently there developed an attempt to free economic life from governmental control. For a time the cause of democracy and the cause of free enterprise were viewed as one and the same. But no longer is this the case. The freedom thus won for economic operations has given birth to strong and aggressive economic groups that recognize no ethical claim superior to their own interests. Individualism in economics fostered and encouraged the growth of powerful, self-governing organizations within the state; virtually governments within the government, that acknowledge no law prior to the urgency of their own concerns. So it is that in Congress many representatives of the people take their instructions from self-seeking groups, a farm bloc or a silver bloc, or a labor bloc. So it was that John L. Lewis and his miners refused in the midst of war to bow to any authority other than their own will even though the exercise of this will threatened to lead to the closing of war industries and the collapse of our armies in the field. Loyalty to a union or a bloc or a narrow interest supersedes loyalty to the country as a whole. Or, more accurately speaking, there is no functioning conception of the country as a whole, or of a public welfare, as something distinct from a collection of competing interests.

Were we to trace the origins for this dangerous state of anarchy, we should locate it ultimately in our traditional notions of the individual as a self-sufficient entity. In this country it derives largely from our Puritan inheritance, from the concept of the soul as essentially alone in the world and dependent for its ultimate salvation upon the execution of conditions imposed upon it by an external and a jealous God. Salvation thus came from the faithful and the literal execution of commandments laid upon man, not from his own inner nature or the merging of his life with others in genuine acts of self-forgetfulness, or from living fruitfully in the lives of his fellows.

The good life was a hard life and a disciplined life—in that it represented in no sense what one really wanted to do but rather what one saw himself compelled and constrained to do. Consequently the moment this outer authority was relaxed, or the authenticity of its preachments challenged, the occasion for the good life disappeared and self-expression easily became license and lack of consideration for others.

It is individualism also that threatens the security of international relationships. Here it appears under the guise of the doctrine of national sovereignty; a state of affairs in which national governments are viewed as something distinct from their people, or the essential concerns and welfare of a people. Governments accordingly are thought of as separate and insulated entities, jealous and independent, endowed with sacred interests and national honors that can yield to no law other than their own arbitrary and selfish purposes. And whereas the agents of the people of one country might normally encounter no obstacles in devising binding arrangements for cooperative endeavor with other peoples along the line of common interests, the sovereign governments, conceived as something apart from these selfsame people, are not so easily persuaded to impair their self-sufficiency.

With what results? That the peoples of the earth are today deprived of all means other than war with which to curb the lust of one sovereign power for the possessions of another.

As the world becomes more closely knit there is danger that disaster will overtake us unless we reformulate the basic assumptions we live by. Modern man dwells in an interdependent world. When the Japanese seized the East Indies, American rubber supplies dried up. When the Nazis embarked upon a ruthless and brutal campaign against the Jews, anti-Semitism and allied intolerances spread as a deadly poison throughout American civil, economic and political life. Nor can we acquiesce longer in the hoary liberal principle that each man in a free society may act as he will provided only he interfere not with a similar privilege for another. The free society of today is an interlocking society. It requires of its members an active concern one for the other. No nation can longer live unto itself alone. Men's lives interpenetrate in subtle as well as obvious ways.

By what principle, then, shall they control their lives?

To this we reply, "Strive to transform the facts of interdependence into an ideal of fruitful interrelationships. Conceive of men as necessary one to the other. Adopt as a principle of action a constructive tolerance and a way of life in which each seeks to promote that which is best in himself by making of it a condition for the distinctive development of his fellows."

This principle assumes that men differ from each other in many respects but that they can be made nevertheless to enrich and supplement each other. Variety thus becomes not merely the spice but the meat of life. Our principle also tests the successful performance of duty—that of husband toward wife, of child to parent, of citizen to his government or of practitioner to his profession and vocation—by the degree to which each succeeds in stimulating others to use their lives more fruitfully. For example, the parent fulfills his function as parent not by persuading his child to follow in his own footsteps, but by observing the peculiar talents of his child and stimulating him to develop them in his own way. Likewise a teacher's professional growth consists in a steadily maturing insight into the needs of his students and a constantly improved skill in serving these needs. The same is true of other vocations. In each instance true success is measured by the degree to which one function furthers a corresponding unique expression of function in others.

This theory denies the validity of certain commonly held views that promote conflict between individuals and groups. It refuses to admit that labor and capital are fundamentally opposed, and it rejects utterly the concept of class conflict that seems to have permeated present-day society. It holds rather that intelligence and good will and imagination can devise ways for capital and labor to cooperate helpfully when both conceive of work as concerned with more than wages and profits and seek to pool their resources for a mutual enhancement of the quality of living.

And need we add that our concept of mutuality in living can be used to promote friendly interrelationships between nations, in contrast with the rivalry of national sovereignties of today? Indeed, it refuses to consider either national or international governments as something foreign and apart from the people they serve. It reminds us that the familiar dictum, "the best government is one that governs least," is an inheritance from the period in which the governing class as a class used its position of power in order to exploit the governed. A democratic government, on the other hand, is an agency that people devise and employ with a view to performing certain tasks that lend themselves best to cooperative endeavor. An interdependent world is dependent upon both national and international agencies for the realization of common ends. These means and these ends are altogether different from the traditional rivalries between national sovereignties. They serve rather to utilize specific ways in which the interests of one people impinge upon the interests of another in the furtherance of cooperative living as between all who dwell on the earth.

The principle of human worth and the assumption that we live best when we identify our lives with others, suggests a third principle, the acceptance of cultural diversity as the only sound basis for lasting peace between peoples.

Lawrence K. Frank, writing on "World Order and Cultural Diversity,"[3] has stated, only too accurately, that Western European culture, which we share with the nations stemming from Egyptian, Greek, Judaic, and Roman backgrounds, tends to ignore or deny the value and significance of other cultures. Toward the peoples of ancient lands—India, China, Japan, Africa—many of whom have cultural traditions, religions, philosophies, and ways of life far more ancient than ours, we have manifested smug complacency and often outright disdain. We conceive of ourselves as the "master race," natively endowed with superior wisdom and enlightenment and entitled therefore to impose our ideas and religions, our institutions and social practices, as well as our political and economic controls upon the less progressive races. Colonization and empire, missionary zeal and economic exploitation are predicated upon this assumption. Like the classical Greeks we regard those who speak a different tongue and attempt to order their lives on a different design, as barbarians, to be pitied for their benighted condition or exploited and degraded when they block the path of those who bear the "white man's burden"! Hitler's brutal doctrine of a German master race reveals in stark ruthlessness what Western European culture has long accepted as a major premise. The sordid history of our relations with the colored races testifies eloquently to the operation of this premise in diplomacy, economics, and even religion.

[3] An article in *Free World* for June, 1942. Also printed in *Frontiers of Democracy*, Vol. IX, October, 1942, pp. 12–14.

The war should bring home to us with dramatic emphasis the dangers in these assumptions of superiority. Have not the Nazis demonstrated the tragic conclusions to which this superiority complex may lead? The ruthless extinction of minorities who refuse to accept slavery and large scale transfers of populations as a logical means for insuring homogeneity?

Each of us can align himself against minor evils of parochialism, but the positive generation of tolerant attitudes toward cultural differences is less easily promoted. It requires more than mutual adjustment and understanding with respect to divergencies in names and customs, difficult as this is to effect, since differences in manners are frequently more irritating and consequently more conducive to intolerance than are differences in morals! It necessitates as well the accommodation of philosophies of life to each other; the surrender of all claims to the possession of an exclusive road to salvation; the recognition, as a condition of living peacefully with others, that there may be more than one true faith.

How difficult it is to accept cultural diversity in the realm of religion and philosophy becomes clear when we peruse recent literature on the democratic way of life. Here we encounter repeatedly the assertion that democracy is conditioned upon the acceptance of the religious interpretation of life peculiar to western man. There is not only considerable agreement in this literature with the contention of one writer that "a democracy completely divorced from religious sanction many Americans would not understand,"[4] but also a tendency to ground democracy in a narrow parochial outlook.

It is essential for us to recognize that the sources of democracy are plural; nor can we safely condone today parochial interpretations of its possibilities. The conviction that democ-

[4] Justin W. Nixon, "The Moral Basis of Democracy" in *Science, Philosophy and Religion* (Third Symposium). New York: Published by Conference on Science, Philosophy and Religion in Relation to the Democratic Way of Life, 1943.

racy, in order to survive, requires the exclusive acceptance of any one philosophical or religious or racial dogma is fraught with danger.

Far wiser is it to orient thinking along the lines suggested by Lawrence K. Frank in the article to which we have referred. In this article Dr. Frank points out that despite all "differences in size, shape, color and in some physiological functions, man as a species is essentially alike everywhere." Everywhere also he encounters certain persistent tasks of life: to gain food, clothing, shelter, security, to organize some form of group life, to regulate human conduct by transforming impulsive behavior into standards and codes and methods of living cherished by a group. As a means for accomplishing and refining these ends he has evolved certain assumptions about himself, about nature and the world; and out of these assumptions have emerged his religions, his philosophies, his art, his differing political, social and economic institutions. These constitute the tools he would employ for solving his persistent problems.

Quite naturally, then, each philosophy, religion, way of life represents certain valuable insights into man's nature and his needs, as it embodies suggestions on how best to meet these needs. But it reveals as well, upon inspection, severe limitations. It is partial. It has its blind spots. This suggests as one condition of world peace a humbleness of spirit on the part of all cultural groups regarding the merits of their ways of life. Nor is our western culture an exception to the rule. It has its contributions to add to the totality of cultures but we cannot assume *a priori* that it is superior as such or more sacredly grounded. Whether or no the nations of the earth will seek to drink from its springs in order to find refreshment will depend upon what it promises for them in rich and meaningful living rather than upon the extraneous power and force it can muster.

Does this leave us in a state of cultural anarchy? With no more uniting bond than a general spirit of tolerance?

Again, no. As Alexander Meiklejohn has shown,[5] there are two attitudes we may characterize as tolerant. One springs from despair, the other from hope. The tolerance of despair "accepts differences of belief as final, as irreducible. It regards the minds of men not as working together but as working separately and independently." This goes no further than to say, "I will agree not to interfere with your belief if you will agree not to interefere with mine." It leaves men at best to live and work together in an atomistic, individualistic world—as untouchables might agree upon a *modus vivendi*.

The second conception of toleration is hopeful. It regards men as working in a common cause; "as they use their minds, individuals or groups are grappling with a common problem. Each of them, working with his own powers and his own materials, makes such contribution as he can to the common task. And when they find their separate intellectual results opposing one another, they recognize that each must take account of what the other is doing." Their differences are thus "of value in pointing the way which all alike must travel if the common work is to be done."

It is this positive tolerance that constitutes a basis for creating a world community out of the present tragic international situation. But to positive toleration we should add, as an essential principle for all to employ, an affirmative faith in man and his inventiveness; a faith sufficiently optimistic to embrace possibilities beyond and in excess of any parochial answers thus far made to life's meaning; a faith that man's potentialities for generous and creative living exceed any temporary or momentary expression of these potentialities.

Such a faith can be, and has been, grounded in supernaturalistic sanction,—as when religious adherents of the Social Gospel movement have sought divine sanction for an optimistic conception of human nature and of their active hope for creating a Kingdom of God on earth. This movement,

[5] *Education Between Two Worlds,* pp. 58–59. New York: Harper & Brothers, 1943.

indeed, but follows in the footsteps of countless individuals who have through the centuries looked to a God in the Heavens or beyond space and time to sustain their noblest aspirations for improving man's lot.

But this faith can also be grounded humanistically, naturalistically. Men conclude all too frequently that skepticism with regard to supernaturalism deprives them of logical grounds for living a good life and reduces them to the level of the beasts of the field. Nothing is more false. As Alexander Meiklejohn puts it,

> The truth is . . . human prophets have perceived in human nature itself the beauty of holiness, the strength of humility, the magnificence of wisdom. And these qualities seemed to them so great, so significant in their authority over the beliefs and the conduct of men that, without knowing what they were doing, they created the myths of divine origins and divine sanctions. That myth is now fading away. But the human truth to which it gave untenable expression still remains. Courage, beauty, freedom, justice, honesty, are still the original facts. The myth was the secondary thing.

Nor is this humanistic faith evidence of inordinate "pride and egoism." On the contrary, it is one with an essential humbleness of spirit, a willingness to concede that it possesses no monopoly upon truth, a recognition that truth and goodness are ever in process of evolution, that the insights and the achievements of one group of people, of one nation, or of one race, are but partial views, requiring supplementation and often reconstruction with changes in time and circumstance;—it testifies to that "meekness of spirit" which the Scriptures assure us is designed ultimately to inherit the earth.

 A fourth essential in the free man's faith is the conviction that man is primarily responsible for his own fate. He believes that the culture in which we live is a product of creative effort in a contest with nature and the circumstances of men's lives.

This is an ancient point of view, yet novel in its implications for the future. The Greeks first formulated it in their dramas. Then it was forgotten; and all through the ages men have tended to hold something other than themselves responsible for the society of their own creation. If we once realize that our society has actually evolved out of the efforts of men there is no excuse for yielding to overwhelming pessimism. Indeed we have every right to be thrilled at the wonderful character of our achievements. Only when we believe that men have fallen from a prior state of perfection need there be cause for discouragement. Once we accept the fact that man creates his society, we can view his worst failures as no more than temporary lapses. Against these backslidings and reversions to the primitive, we may contrast his extraordinary progress through the ages. And with this record to encourage us we can set our faces resolutely to the future.

For some years, as a young man, William James corresponded with a friend, Thomas W. Ward, who evidently entered business much against his wishes. Ward was a sensitive man, discouraged and gloomy over his lot. James, at the time, was fighting against a breakdown and an agony of uncertainty as to how to steer his own life. The letters written by James under these trying circumstances can bring strength and assurance to anyone who is undergoing severe personal trial.[6]

One letter, in particular, is worth quoting in connection with our insistence that man should depend upon man and the resources of man for comfort and inspiration. Ward had spoken in an exceptionally gloomy vein. In reply, James regrets the "inward deadness and listlessness" into which Ward had fallen but bids him, "Bate not a jot of heart nor hope, but steer right on." After advising Ward in some detail how to combat a temperament from which he must make up his mind "to expect twenty times as much anguish as other people need to get along with," he suggests a more philo-

[6] *Letters of William James.* Boston: The Atlantic Monthly Press, 1920. The letters to Ward to which I refer are in Volume I, p. 130.

sophic basis upon which to ground confidence in himself and people in general. At our lowest ebb, he writes, there is the empirical fact that men suffer and enjoy. Each of us can thus engage in activities that enable us to enter into real relations with our brothers. From this at least one may gather the assurance

that, without what you have done, some individuals must needs be acting now in a somewhat different manner. You have modified their life; you are in *real* relation with them; you have in so far forth entered into their being.

With this as a basis, James puts the question:

And is that such an unworthy stake to set up as our good, after all? Who are these men anyhow? Our predecessors, even apart from the physical link of generation, have made us what we are. Every thought you now have and every act and intention owes its complexion to the acts of your dead and living brothers. *Everything* we know and are is through men. We have no revelation but through man. Every sentiment that warms your gizzard, every brave act that ever made your pulse bound and your nostril open to a confident breath was a man's act. However mean a man may be, man is *the best we know*: and your loathing as you turn from what you probably call the vulgarity of human life—your homesick yearning for a *Better*, somewhere— is furnished by your manhood; your ideal is made up of traits suggested by past men's words and actions. Your manhood shuts you in forever, bounds all your thoughts like an overarching sky—and all the Good and True and High and Dear that you know by virtue of sharing in it. They are the Natural Product of our Race. So that it seems to me that a sympathy with men as such, and a desire to contribute to the weal of a species, which, whatever may be said of it, contains All that we acknowledge as good, may very well form an external interest sufficient to keep one's moral pot boiling in a very lively manner to a good old age.[7]

This sense of kinship with our fellows, so ably expressed by James, has one practical value. It prompts us to weigh and appraise all measures designed to enlist the self-sacrifice and

[7] *Ibid.*, p. 131.

the loyalty of people by their discernible effects upon the quality of men's lives. It commits us to the principle that the measure of all measures is man.

The insistence that man is the measure of all measures does not mean, as so often charged, that the higher values of life are equated with a mess of pottage; nor that long-term considerations will surrender to the immediate and the most urgent. It implies merely that human beings should strive to attain manhood stature in the realm of moral theory and moral behavior. Nor is it so much a question of how we shall conceive the ultimate nature of man; that is, whether we shall view him as the noblest work of God or as the product of a long period of evolution in which he has rough-hewn all that we cherish and value; whether he be merely a messenger bearing witness to the worthiness he possesses or a dignitary in his own right.

In either case we hold with James that "Everything we know and are is through man"; and we insist that every proposal to lift up the eyes of the people unto the hills or to improve their ways be appraised in terms of its ultimate effect upon the quality of living. In sum, we are concerned first and last with people and with a communion between people. As John Lovejoy Elliott once stated:

We hold . . . that communion can be established between men by the powers native in them. We shall not rise to the full perception of our task until we regard all of the essential relationships of men to each other as a kind of communion, as much a sacrament as any communion symbolized in earlier religions. It is to give that quality to all the relations of men that we exist. Only as we strive effectually to create that quality in daily living, in our group relationships as well as in our personal dealings, can we enter fully into the fellowship of the ethical life, can we share in its work with the sense that perhaps here we touch the things that are highest.[8]

Thus it remains true as of old that he who would save his soul must ever be ready to lose it!

[8] "The Basis of Ethical Fellowship." Pamphlet issued by Society for Ethical Culture, 2 West 64 Street, New York City.

PART II

*

CHAPTER IV

What Is This Education for Freedom?

AT a recent meeting in New York City the Congress of American Industry reaffirmed the faith of American business men in free enterprise. One overly-enthusiastic advocate of unrestricted enterprise, an executive vice-president of the National Association of Manufacturers, stressed the pre-established harmony that he sees existing between individual motive and general welfare. Said he,

That's the nice thing about our social and economic set-up here in America. Everyone concentrates on getting what he wants for himself, but finds that the only way he can do it is by providing others with things they want enough to be willing to buy and pay for. We don't have to be philanthropists. We can be selfish as all hell and still find that, unless we can fool the police, we can't get something without giving something in return.[1]

This speaker characterized the depression period in which the Federal government strove to assist the unemployed as "the lush days of manna from the Potomac," and reaffirmed his confidence in "justice" not "benevolence." In this he joined hands with still another speaker who assured us that America "promises to every individual a full reward deter-mined by his productivity; and it cannot give him that by making him 'share the wealth' with the unproductive."

It is significant (some will say ominous) that this over-simplified faith in an individualism that endorses *laissez faire* in business and industry and frowns upon the use of govern-

[1] Quoted in *Information Service*, January 22, 1944, publication of Federal Council of the Churches of Christ in America (Department of Research and Education), 297 Fourth Ave., New York City.

ment in order to ward off misfortune coincides with an equally vigorous reassertion of eighteenth century thought in education. This educational movement has taken as its slogan the title of a book written by President Hutchins, "Education for Freedom," and has set about to reform American schools and colleges by reverting to the kind of education that, we are told by one of its members, disappeared in the early part of the nineteenth century.

This group, "Education for Freedom," condemns the prevailing curriculum in schools and colleges. If we may judge from the statements of its leading exponents, it would substitute uniform, required subjects for attempts to minister to individual differences and needs. It deplores the correlation of vocational and general education. Attempts to relate the school to life, to enrich the curriculum with first-hand experience, or to promote character development through "learning by doing" it indicts as shallow and superficial pedagogy. Indeed, these modern trends are directly charged with responsibility for the crisis that now grips American life. Therefore, if we would save America, we are warned, we must transform our education. "Education for Freedom," thus requires a right-about-face in the work of our schools and colleges. Let us ring out the new and ring in the old!

Before turning to the positive program of this counter-reformation, we shall consider in more detail the criticism it directs against contemporary education.

II

First is the frequent charge that our schools do not develop the rudimentary arts of an education. As one speaker charged in a radio address, "Reading, writing and arithmetic were thrown out of secondary schools, and in their stead were introduced manual training, domestic science, typewriting, and a host of similar subjects which we wanted our children to have and which we insisted our school boards give us." Consequently, it is concluded, our young people cannot read, figure, or write. Thus do they lack the essential arts of communication obviously basic in a free society.

This indictment is not peculiar to this group. Nor is it the unique possession of contemporary critics of the school. Indeed, were we to appraise American education by means of criticisms· alone, we should conclude that generation by generation the work of our schools has become progressively worse!

Fortunately the facts do not sustain this inference. Anyone who wishes to consult the data yielded by patient investigation, as against the partial reports blazoned forth in newspaper headline, will discover to his amazement that the results of instruction have improved steadily rather than the opposite; and, oddly enough, that progressive schools succeed better than the old-fashioned and conventional institution. These data indicate, moreover, that in all the fundamental processes—reading, writing, arithmetic—the children of today are mastering operations at a much *earlier chronological age* than ever before and with a proficiency superior to that of the olden day.

These facts were clearly established in an exhaustive investigation conducted more than twenty years ago by Caldwell and Courtis, and published in their volume *Then and Now in Education*. The authors resurrected examinations given to school children in Boston in 1845, and subjected children of our day to these same tests. Despite the fact that in the 1840's only superior pupils were privileged to present themselves for examination, and that the children examined by Caldwell and Courtis constituted a run-of-the-mine group, the children of the 1920's were clearly superior in their performance to those of 1845.

One difference between the emphasis in the teaching of yesterday and of today was made clear, however; a difference most important to bear in mind when we seek to measure the tangible results of instruction. Caldwell and Courtis remarked, "Present-day children tend to make lower scores on the pure memory and abstract skill questions and higher scores on the thought or meaningful questions."[2]

These conclusions coincide with the results of a recent study of the records of graduates from progressive schools in college when contrasted with those of graduates of conventional schools. So, too, do they agree with the conclusions of the Commission on American History (representing a group of historical associations in this country). The Commission states: "If by knowing history one means the ability to recall dates, names, and specific events, the answer is fairly clear: Americans in general do not know this kind of history. If by knowing history one means the understanding of trends and movements, the appreciation of past events, persons, and the ability to see a connection between the experience of the country and the experience of the individual, the answer is that Americans in general do know a reasonable amount of American history."[3]

There is ample evidence from comparative studies to indicate that the schools of today lay far more stress than did those of yesterday upon helping children to understand and utilize in their daily lives the information and the skills they acquire, and there is ample evidence, in addition, that the contemporary student is as proficient as were his forebears in speedily forgetting what seems to him irrelevant and useless for his purposes!

Does this mean that we are satisfied with the work of our schools? By no means! It suggests merely that much of the criticism leveled against schools and colleges lacks perspective and, frequently, evidence of those self-same qualities of mind and character the critics would have our educational institu-

---

[2] *Op. cit.*, p. 85. Yonkers-on-Hudson, New York: World Book Co., 1924.

[3] *American History in Schools and Colleges*, the Report of the Committee on American History in Schools and Colleges of the American History Association, the Mississippi Valley Historical Association, The National Council of the Social Studies, p. 1. New York: The Macmillan Company, 1944.

tions instill. Nothing is more deplorable, for example, than the shot-gun type of indictment directed of late against the products of progressive education, particularly the common tendency to use the results of general surveys of schools which offend against everything the progressive stands for as evidence of the pernicious influence of his principles and his practices.

But the indictment of "Education for Freedom" cuts deeper than the mere failure of schools to develop skill in reading, writing, and arithmetic. It charges them with responsibility for the crisis in contemporary civilization. As Mark Van Doren states, "Education for Freedom, in other words, traces the troubles of our civilization back to you and me as individuals. It is we and hundreds of millions like us, who must learn to manage our understanding and desire. The question in large part is the question of education."

Nor is this merely a failure to manage understanding and desire in a broad and general sense. The schools and colleges are charged with direct responsibility for neglecting the indispensable content of an education that might have saved America from specific errors of judgment.

For example, Stringfellow Barr, in an article in the *New Republic* of August 31, 1942 and again in the *Magazine Digest* of November, 1943, contends that but for the curriculum of our schools and colleges America would have avoided grave errors of judgment such as our delay in entering the war and our general failure to appreciate the merits of Streit's plan for "Union Now!" These specific errors, he argues, which sprout from an erring education as weeds in a neglected garden follow from the false intellectual premises on which our educational institutions are operating. These premises which "we were teaching the next generation, were demonstrably false and were logically leading towards a smash-up." To save America, one thing is imperative,—restore to the colleges "the kind of education in the liberal arts which many American colleges had furnished well into the nineteenth century."[4]

President Hutchins agrees with Van Doren and Barr in the remedy they prescribe, but he is more moderate in his judgment of the school's role in corrupting American society. For example, in his recent volume, *Education for Freedom*, Hutchins points out that the times and not the schools are out of joint, since educational systems can do no more than reflect the culture of which they are a part.

Hutchins believes the besetting sin of American life is materialism—"The doctrine by which we have lived is that material goods are an end in themselves." This materialism accounts for the major ills of school and college education. The love of money, as exemplified in the search for endowments and gifts, the dependence upon student fees and legislative grants, have led to a service station conception of education. It prompts course offerings designed to appease pressure groups and to attract large numbers of students. It leads inevitably to practical and vocational courses and ends with an equating of the values of an education with superficial criteria for success in life. From these errors it is but a step to specific ills in education: the prevalence of an elective system, wherein one thing is considered as important as another; the inclusion of vocational training in general education; the substitution of information for sound values and the rigorous training of the mind.

Materialism thus rules supreme. "It has captured the state. It has captured education."

Can we be saved? Yes, Hutchins believes, but only by a near miracle and a profound change of heart. If we can be persuaded to introduce anew an education that places first virtue and intelligence, the training of the intellect, there is a fighting chance of regenerating American society. "If one

[4] "The Education of Freemen," *The New Republic*, August 31, 1942, pp. 248–250.

college and one university—and only one—are willing to take a position contrary to the prevailing American ideology and suffer the consequences, then conceivably, over a long period of time, the character of our civilization may change."

Oddly enough, Walter Lippmann aligns himself with Barr rather than with Hutchins in a resounding condemnation of our educational system. In an address entitled "Education and Western Civilization" delivered in the spring of 1941 to the Phi Beta Kappa Society, he put forth the following theses:

1. That during the past forty or fifty years those responsible for education have progressively removed from the curriculum of studies the Western culture which produced the modern democratic state;
2. That the schools and colleges have, therefore, been sending out into the world men who no longer understand the creative principle of the society in which they live;
3. That deprived of their cultural tradition, the newly educated Western men no longer possess in the form and substance of their minds and spirits, the ideas, the premises, the rationale, the logic, the method, the values or the deposited wisdom which are the genius of the development of Western civilization;
4. That the prevailing education is destined, if it continues, to destroy Western civilization and is in fact destroying it.

5. Consequently, Lippmann pleads for a "thorough reconsideration of the underlying assumptions" and purposes of this education. The need for this reconsideration causes Lippmann to insist upon an education designed to restore faith in the religious and cultural heritage of the past. Thus he states:

The institutions of the Western world were formed by men who learned to regard themselves as inviolable persons because they were rational and free. They meant by rational that they were capable of comprehending the moral order of the universe and their place in the moral order. They meant that when they regarded themselves as free that within that order they had a personal moral responsibility to perform their duties and to exercise their corresponding rights. From this conception of the unity of mankind in a rational order, the Western world has derived its conception of law, which is that all men and all communities of men and all authority among men are subject to law, and that the character of all particular laws is to be judged by whether they conform to or violate, approach or depart from the rational order of the universe and of man's nature.

These are strong words, written as they are by a man whose *Preface to Morals* differs utterly from the above in its analysis and in its prescription for the confusions of modernity. Are Lippmann's words to be taken literally? Surely no one knows better than he that the specific philosophical and religious foundations upon which the notion of a "rational order of the universe and of man's nature" once rested are gone forever. Does he seriously suggest that we should teach young people, as Jefferson and the men who wrote the American Constitution and the Bill of Rights were taught, the doctrine of natural law and Cicero's principle of right reason? Or that we should turn their minds back, as from darkness unto light, to the assumption of Thomas Aquinas that rational creatures are rational because they participate in "The Eternal Law of God"? Or "impart," to use Lippmann's term, a faith in John Locke's state of nature from which the rights of life, liberty, and "estate" derive? Can this be what he means by imparting the tradition of western civilization as a basis for the solution of our democratic ills?

At least one member of "Education for Freedom" insists upon a more forthright analysis of the evils within modern education and a more creative solution of its ills. We refer to Alexander Meiklejohn who holds that teaching, both British and American, has lost its sanity. But he does not attribute the causes of this disease to mere changes in the curriculum of school and college in the past forty or fifty years. As Meiklejohn sees it, our difficulties go back to what Lippmann once termed the "acids of modernity," to the fact that

for three centuries our Protestant-Capitalist culture, which has dominated the modern world, has been in process of disintegration. Both Protestantism and Capitalism have been working toward a denial of their own presuppositions. And especially in England and the United States our cultural disintegration has been moving on to a culminating and desperate crisis.

This disintegrating process reveals itself most clearly in education because Anglo-American schools and colleges were founded on precisely the principles to which Barr and Lippmann and Hutchins would have them renew their loyalty! Thus, he continues,

Anglo-American schools and colleges were established primarily on a basis of religious faith. They expressed a belief in the Mind and Will of God. And that belief gave unity to knowledge. It gave unity to human action and to the intelligence which guided action. It united knowledge and intelligence one to another. When men sought after truth or goodness in any field whatever, they were tracing the well-integrated pattern of that Divine Mind-Will in whose image they themselves had been made. Our God was one God. In Him was One Truth and One Righteousness. In Him all the intellectual multiplicities, all the practical impulses and strains of the human scene were taken up into a unity of meaning and purpose. That unity dominated or was intended to dominate the whole course of teaching. It gave guidance to teachers and pupils alike. Young people learned, and were taught, as children of God.[5]

But, states Meiklejohn, this world view is dead and gone. Consequently the challenge confronting education today is to create unity out of a new faith in the brotherhood of man. This requires the construction of a new underpinning for this faith, in full realization that "human morality has no cosmic backing," but is rather "whatever men make it to be." This faith, as we have indicated, grounds itself in the brotherhood of man and in man's capacity to exercise reason; that is, to learn "to regard the interests of any other person as of equal importance with one's own" and "to love one's neighbor as oneself." Reason, in Meiklejohn's plan, is thus social

[5] "Reason and Violence," *Common Sense*, Vol. XII, August, 1943, pp. 283–286.

and emotional as well as intellectual. It is forward looking, not backward in its reference. It uses the past with a view to its import for the future, not as a sacred residue of fixed truths that young people can discover only by means of an esoteric method.

It must be added, however, that Meiklejohn is one with his colleagues in the positive program they propose. In his volume, *Education Between Two Worlds*, he advocates the substitution of the authority of the state in education for the worn-out authority of religion. He also believes that general education should be uniform for all students. This follows from his conviction that the peculiar function of a liberal arts college is to teach for "intelligence," by which he means a power capable of effective application in any field whatsoever. And, finally, he endorses the curriculum of the "Great Books" on the ground that, to his knowledge, it is the most promising suggestion in the field at present for reorganizing the liberal arts curriculum.

So much for the indictment that "Education for Freedom" directs against contemporary education. What of the positive program?

III

Most spectacular, of suggested reforms, is the attempt of St. John's College to organize the undergraduate period of college around one hundred of the great books of western civilization. These books are grouped in both a historical and a disciplinary sequence. When organized chronologically they fall into four cultural periods, one period for the work of each year of a four-year course. From a disciplinary point of view they are classified into three groups: one designed to teach the arts of reading, understanding, and criticism; one primarily literary and linguistic; one mathematical and scientific.

Incidentally, *The Federalist Papers*, the *Constitution of the United States*, and William James' *Principles of Psychology* seemingly constitute a sufficient introduction to the culture and civilization of the Americas!

This plan, we are assured, represents a restoration of the liberal arts to American education; a return to the trivium and quadrivium of the mediaeval university, when education, in President Barr's words, "was concerned, and solely concerned, with cultivating through discipline the intellectual powers of young men."

But was it? To a student of the original content of the trivium and the quadrivium, the hundred great books will come with as much surprise as to the uninitiated layman. On the one hand, we are assured that the liberal arts constitute an indispensable subject matter and a specific method, comprising the original curriculum of school and college, which it is proposed to bring back into American education. From this and this alone, it is argued, can young people acquire the ideas and the logic essential for free men in a democratic society. And, presto! we are confronted with a novel curriculum consisting of an arbitrary number of books selected to be taught in a manner known only to the laborers in the vineyard of St. John's!

In defense of this experiment, it may be suggested, as Mark Van Doren has in fact suggested, that the trivium and the quadrivium should be reinterpreted to mean in the one case the discipline of reading, writing, and thinking (trivium) and in the other mathematics and science. In other words, the liberal arts are flexible and variable in substance.

Many will agree that this is as it should be, since, in plain fact, both the subject matter and the methods of the seven liberal arts have undergone evolution in the course of the centuries. But what does this imply with respect to an arbitrary content of education that must be uniform and required of all students? Once the principle of relativity is applied to the substance and the procedures of the trivium and the quadrivium, may we not conclude as well, what these reformers are eager to deny, that educational values do not reside as such in any arbitrary subject matter, but originate rather out of the interplay of the experiences of the individual student with materials and methods, relevant and appropriate to his abilities and needs! And when we seek to explore the full implications of this observation, will not a uniform prescription in education suffer the same fate as patent nostrums for universal ills in the field of medicine?

This reference to uniform prescriptions suggests a second plank in the platform of "Education for Freedom." Under the caption of "education for all" it proposes to eliminate the elective system from colleges and all curricular provisions in secondary school and college alike that respect differences in talent and future plans. It would cast out all courses involving vocational exploration as well as vocational training and in place of a differentiated curriculum it would require a uniform curriculum for all students below the graduate school.

Now most educators recognize the need for common, integrating experiences that will unite students in certain basic ideas and ideals and develop common attitudes and dispositions. Particularly is this essential if a shared democratic culture is to evolve out of variegated racial and religious backgrounds of the peoples now composing our population. Indeed few will deny that an educational system, from elementary school through college and university, has already done much to create unity out of racial diversity. Nevertheless any suggestion in these days of renewed tension that we educate for what is common to all men receives a sympathetic ear.

But let it be as well a critical ear! For by *common human nature*, "Education for Freedom" means a metaphysical essence in man quite different in substance and character from what we ordinarily conceive of as shared experiences or the social product of intimate association in common enterprises. Obviously ideals such as respect for differences, the concept of "Americans all" with equal rights before the law, or the principle that men will realize themselves most adequately when they use their special abilities to enhance distinctiveness in the lives of others, can originate out of and receive confirmation in a variety of experiences. For one a story or a poem, an historical incident or philosophical tract, will bring insight. Another will be touched more quickly and profoundly through the medium of the arts, a picture, sculptured figure, or music. Still a third responds more sensitively to the living touch that comes from working or playing with others in concrete situations. In each case, however, the recognition of the brotherhood of man and the vision of our common nature imply a quality of relationship with people, an interpenetration of life with life that men can and do in fact experience.

But this is not the common nature of "Education for Freedom." Common nature as thus conceived is a substance or an essence in man, not a potential relationship or association. It is a faculty of the mind or reason containing within itself slumbering ideas or principles, that only one kind of subject matter or discipline can bring into being. When this distinction between common nature as an outgrowth of cooperative relationships and common nature as a substance in which all men share is made clear, statements such as the following take on quite a different meaning for education than a first superficial reading suggests. The quotation is from Mark Van Doren's *Liberal Education*:

> Aldous Huxley calls liberal education abstract. If he means that it is general, or occupied with a nature always assumed to be the same, then he is right. . . . In these pages it is still to be defined, but when the moment comes for that it should already be clear that liberal education is nothing less than the complete education of men as men; it is the education of persons; or, ideally, it is education.[6]

The concern to educate what is common in man prompts "Education for Freedom" to revive two questionable as-

[6] P. 29. New York: Henry Holt and Co., 1944.

sumptions of teaching: (1) that there is a subject matter for teaching best adapted to convey to all students, without reference to their differences, certain fundamental values, ideas and principles indispensable for an education; and (2) that this subject matter, when properly taught, possesses a magic virtue and can thus develop in students an intellectual power "capable of being applied in any field whatever."

The educators have a name for these two assumptions. Some fifty years ago they were characterized as formal discipline. At that time this theory of mental discipline blocked the way of efforts to liberalize the curriculum on behalf of the needs of boys and girls of varied abilities and life goals who were beginning to find in a free education the open sesame to American life.

Did you question, for example, that Mary should continue her mathematics or her Latin because the content of the subject was foreign to her background and her intentions, as well as her ability, you were assured that while this might be true, nevertheless there was a discipline, a general intellectual power that Mary must of necessity derive from this material and this material alone. On the other hand, if you demonstrated that the intellectual power thus identified did not in fact transfer to Mary, then were you persuaded that there was an invaluable content within the disputed subject that all should possess. Only after painstaking research and laboratory experiment were Edward L. Thorndike and other psychologists successful in disproving the validity of formal discipline as applied to both content and method. Were we to return to this antiquated notion of the mind and of educational values, we should indeed wipe out the good with the bad in modern education.

The fact is, as we have suggested earlier, whether or not a subject of study gives rise to either ideas or disciplined ways of thinking, depends upon the kind of relationship established between the learner and this subject.

Nor is there anything mysterious about this observation.

We all know how a book, or a poem, or an experience on the street may deeply move or profoundly transform the outlook of one man at the same time that it leaves another cold.

Consider, for example, the following incident which the distinguished architect, Robert D. Kohn, relates of his education. He was a young student, studying abroad.

As a youngster my interests were primarily in the arts of design. I knew no history except the usual American history and sketchy grammar school Greek and Roman history; knew that these periods were followed by "dark ages" and then the Renaissance. But at the same period I could identify at sight whether a piece of sculpture or carving was Greek or Roman or "Romanesque" or Gothic or Renaissance—and what was more, I could identify its country of origin.

At one end of the terrace of the mediaeval castle of Amboise in France there was a low stone doorway, gothic in form against the head of which, the guide told us Charles VIII had struck his head and so died in 1498. The ornaments at the top of the doorway were gothic but down the sides were panels of carving—as I now remember showing in the upper part the influence of the classic revival on the French stone cutters in the time of Louis XII. But towards the bottom of these same panels the ornaments and the cutting were Italian—just like the work I had seen illustrated on Florentine tombs of twenty years earlier date. But here was carving started by Frenchmen and finished by Italians! What happened in the early years of the 16th century between France and Italy to have resulted in this strange sequence? Then, too, at the other end of that same terrace there was a late gothic chapel in which they said were buried the bones of Leonardo da Vinci, whom Francis the First had induced to come to France and who died there in 1519.

Well, I would have to know something about the historical relations between France and Italy to account for this interesting carved doorway at Amboise, just as I wanted to know more about the relations of France and England about this same time to know what were the objectives and the results of that Field of the Cloth of Gold (1520) I had seen carved on the walls of Rouen's Town Hall.

So I began to read European history.

From years of experience it has been found that when the teachers of science, or history, or language, or the arts or what not, select and organize the materials within these fields with reference to the interests of their students, intellectual thoroughness and eagerness is accentuated rather than retarded.

We do not conclude from this that we should resort to individual instruction, or that some subjects and some materials within a given subject are no better than others. It is rather to hold that teaching is a profession and that school and college as well as the individual teacher will have to use professional judgment, in deciding how far or in what ways young people should share experiences and when it is better to individualize instruction.

There are two extremes in education against which we must be on our guard. One is an undue reaction against the formalism now finding renewed expression in "Education for Freedom." This holds that since the classics, mathematics, language—in short, the trivium and quadrivium—can in fact serve the needs of but a small number, they are to be excluded from an education genuinely concerned with the "masses." This group would overemphasize the immediate and the tangible, and, if left to itself, might well vocationalize our schools with a vengeance. Its limitations and excesses are quite properly condemned as overly materialistic and shortsighted. Were education made over in the image of this ideal, it would snuff out from the lives of many boys and girls intellectual and cultural values that no democracy can do without.

On the other hand, there are people who cannot see that the education they envisage for all would meet the needs of but a few, chiefly the verbally-minded. They exclude altogether the type of mind which, in the words of an English report on education, popularly known as the Norwood report, "has an uncanny insight into the intricacies of mechanism whereas the subtleties of language construction are too delicate"; or still a third type, recognized by the Nor-wood report, that "deals more easily with concrete things than with ideas. He may have much ability, but it will be in the realm of facts. He is interested in things as they are; he finds little attraction in the past or in the slow disentangle-ment of causes and movements."[7]

To refuse to recognize in the curriculum of school and college these genuine differences between young people and the implications for distinctive materials and methods is in-deed to return to a plan of education made in the image of a Procrustean bed.

We thus reject the assumption that there is one subject matter, or one curriculum that can wisely be required of all youth. So, too, we must reject the dogma that powers of mind such as the ability to think with caution and with a sensitiveness to all the facts relevant to a problem, or to devise solutions for novel situations, and to test hypotheses with an eye to all of their implications before putting them into operation, arise exclusively out of one group of subjects or one type of material within these subjects. Consequently we are impelled to warn all commercially minded fathers of ambitious sons to be on their guard against the following words of Stringfellow Barr. President Barr is describing the new curriculum in the liberal arts at St. John's College and is writing in the *Magazine Digest* for November, 1943:

> The man who has learned to practice these arts successfully can "concentrate" on anything, can "apply himself" to anything, can quickly learn any specialty, any profession, any business. That man can deliberate, can make practical decisions by other means than tossing a coin, can understand his failures, can recognize his obligations as well as his opportunities. He is in short what an earlier generation eloquently termed "an educated man."

[7] *Curriculum and Examinations in Secondary Schools*, pp. 2–3. Re-port of the Committee of the Secondary School Examinations Council, appointed by the President of the Board of Education in 1941. London: His Majesty's Stationery Office, 1943.

Who will say what economies will not follow in the operation of our American schools once we convince the restive taxpayer that the educational advantages of schooling are thus directly and immediately related to the contraction of the curriculum?

A third characteristic of "Education for Freedom" is its repudiation of what the friends of modern education call an enriched curriculum and its enemies, fads and frills. As against these new developments we have a vigorous reassertion of, or shall we say reversion to, verbalism.

Despite their failures and their mistakes, progressive schools have influenced contemporary education in two important respects. On the one hand they have emphasized the need of an experiential basis for intellectual and abstract learning, and on the other, they have used the insights of mental hygiene and clinical psychology into child and adolescent development to modify work within both the curricular and extra-curricular activities of the school. Thus have they pointed the way to a more realistic type of learning and a more dynamic character education than formerly.

Speaking broadly this enriched curriculum serves three purposes:

(1) It offsets limitations of experience that might otherwise militate against sound learning. For example, good teachers observe that the ordinary child of today cannot be introduced to arithmetic through exclusively verbal symbols to the extent possible many years ago when elementary children, grade for grade, were older than at present and living experiences outside the school gave repeated illustrations of the meaning of verbal symbols. Thoroughness in learning requires for children and young people alike, the laying of a groundwork in first-hand, concrete, active experience. Nor is this need confined to the mastery of primary arithmetic. It applies to virtually every subject and every age level in school and college alike. It is a consequence that follows upon our artificial and increasingly verbal civilization. Accordingly

we find a number of colleges using field work and work experience quite apart from its money return or its vocational implications in connection with subjects such as economics and sociology; and secondary schools and colleges providing service opportunities for students in agencies outside the school as one means of furthering social maturity as well as intellectual perception.

(2) Secondly, the enriched curriculum enables schools to utilize individual differences on behalf of general education. Conventional provision for individual differences has been restricted to flexible requirements in rate of learning. When all must travel the identical route, the recognition of slow and fast learners is indeed necessary. But this is not sufficient. Individual differences are intelligently cared for only when each student can use his interests and abilities to grasp better the relationship of what he is learning to himself and his world. In the elementary school this involves utilizing art, shop, music, dramatic work and the like as plural routes to learning, with an opportunity for each child to follow that route which promises for him the greatest zest and meaningfulness. On the secondary and college level, subjects of study are profitably viewed as representatives within the school of adult interests outside the school. Toward this end each area—science, art, literature, mathematics, language, what not—can be organized so that it orients students with reference to the vocational, social-civic, cultural world of adults. When successful these out-of-school relationships will bring security and assurance to each student at that critical period in his life when he needs desperately to acquire status in his own eyes and the eyes of others.

(3) Finally, first-hand experience in the life of the school and the community enables educational institutions to give reality to those qualities of character they desire students to acquire. As John Dewey has said, democracy is a moral ideal. When the life of the school brings to expression through the actual participation of students, the ideals we would have

young people live by, we may be certain it functions in moulding character; and this living matrix of relationships constitutes the most effective medium for guiding students into wholesome associations with their fellows.

It is obvious that this type of direct experience adds vitality and reality to education. It is of quite a different order from the overly specific vocational courses to which "Education for Freedom" quite properly objects. And it differs from the miscellaneous offerings which President Hutchins is fond of holding up to ridicule as inane attempts to relate the school to life.

Different as this direct experience is from that ridiculed and abused it is equally condemned.

Today as yesterday, [writes Hutchins] we may leave experience to other institutions and influences and emphasize in education the contribution that it is supremely fitted to make, the intellectual training of the young. The life they lead when they are out of our hands will give them experience enough. We cannot try to give it to them and at the same time perform the task that is ours and ours alone.[8]

To those who have actually observed the regenerative influences upon individuals and communities of rural schools in underprivileged communities, or of institutions such as Tuskegee upon the well-being of a race, or of the recent work of residential centers of the National Youth Administration, or the transformation in neighborhood after neighborhood where faculty and parents have cooperated in an endeavor to "relate school and life," these words of Hutchins sound strangely unreal, as the cloistered observations of a critic who cannot know what he condemns.

So, too, with attempts to organize the total life of the school with an eye to matching better ways of actual living and ideals of living. These are brushed aside with the observation, "since character is the result of choice, it is diffi-

[8] *The Higher Learning in America*, p. 69. New Haven: Yale University Press, 1936.

cult to see how you can develop it unless you train the mind to make intelligent choices."

True, but how do we best train the mind to make intelligent choices? By presenting it with verbal formulations or by helping young people through trial and error in the rough and tumble of their experience to sharpen observation and to refine judgment?

The difficulty traces back again to the conception of mind and of intellectual training "Education for Freedom" would bring back into education. It relies solely upon verbal experience. It contends that training the mind with appropriate materials will insure development of character. It assumes that mind or intelligence conceived as a faculty rather than as a function of the total personality is primary in directing behavior; that thought moulds experience as against the view that experience is the mother of generalizations.

Actually, of course, a good school uses first-hand experience and intellectual activity to reinforce each other. Experience that fails to eventuate in interpretation and is not deepened and enriched by reading is blind; but intellectual experience without taproots in life is equally futile. Let us grant, as we readily do, that many schools in an excess of progressivism have neglected tradition and vigorous intellectual training. But let us likewise inquire how they came thus to sin. Does it not result from the fact that they are reacting unwisely to the barren intellectualism of an earlier day, not unlike that which this counter-reformation would impose once more upon our young people?—Must educators forever confine correction of error to the method of throwing out the baby with the bath?

Finally, we must be on our guard against the nature of the freedom we are told these programs of education will insure. Do we want, even if it were possible, to revert to the past, to train our young people to accept the "rational order of the universe" and of man's nature of which Walter Lippmann speaks? Significant and, indeed, creative as these concepts were for the solution of problems peculiar to the eighteenth century, they fall short of what is required to insure free and liberal relations between men and nations in the twentieth. Long since, the doctrine of *laissez faire* and the principle of enlightened self-interest as a self-sufficient human motive, logical derivatives of the idea of "the rational order of the universe and of man's nature," revealed their inadequacies not merely in the economic order but in personal, social-civic and international relationships as well. As to this suggestion, we are one with Meiklejohn in repudiating it utterly. Men are challenged today to create a new vision of man in relation to his fellows, a vision that is generous not selfish in its fundamental postulates, that insures a genuine brotherhood in an interdependent world.

But it is precisely this atavistic conception of freedom and the free man that seems to characterize the thinking of the school of thought under review. The free man it visualizes will be unhappy in a collectivistic society or a totalitarian state, since he is disciplined to think for himself and to deduce his own conclusions from the truths furnished him by individualistic tradition. But neither is he a citizen of a democracy in which sensitive and responsive personalities seek to enter with sympathy and understanding into the lives of others as a pre-condition of their own self-expression. On the contrary, the ideal envisaged is that of a free individual, concerned, in Van Doren's words, with "one's own excellence, the perfection of one's own intellectual character." The mind trained in this school, is in danger of becoming a denatured reason, a reason which subordinates all passions and all human claims to its logical operations. Such an education may produce the wise but disinterested individual envisaged by Spinoza who, despite the evils that engulf men, "is scarcely at all disturbed in spirit" but "always possesses true acquiescence of his spirit." It is less likely to develop the intelligent and generous men and women of Meiklejohn's vision, who seek earnestly the brotherhood of man. Indeed, we venture to suggest that the enthusiasm with which this movement in American education is received by the crusaders of "free enterprise" testifies to a nostalgic wish on the part of many to escape the obligations of modern life and to return to the free and uncontrolled social and economic order of the past.

And herein consists its danger! A counter-revolution of this character may well sow the seeds of the hurricane.

IV

We conclude that "Education for Freedom" does not insure either an education or a freedom essential for democratic living in an interdependent world. It would have our schools and colleges confuse a part for the whole of their task. All will agree that the training of the intellect is an indispensable aspect of education but we cannot assume that it is in itself sufficient. The free individual, whom we envisage as the end product of a democratic education, is psychologically mature, one in whom emotional and social development have kept pace with the intellectual. As James Marshall wisely remarks,

education should pay greater attention to basic psychological attitudes and drives. . . . The needs of a peaceful world and of a democratic and moral society—a happy land, if you will—require an educational system that will be conscious of psychological motivation and that will have the purpose of developing mature people with mature ends.[9]

Education for psychological maturity will stress no less than does "Education for Freedom" the arts of communication, conceptual thought and the contributions from the past. It recognizes, of course, that men are mutilated and helpless when cut off from their traditions. To know the nature of the problems that have dogged men's progress through the ages and the answers that the wisest and best representatives

[9] "Psychological Maturity as a Basis for Democracy," *Mental Hygiene*, Vol. XXVI, April, 1942, pp. 225–226.

of our race have propounded to these problems, will equip us the better to confront the baffling issues of our day. We cannot know too much history or philosophy if we would employ wisely science and technology to human and humane relationships of living in a society sensitively knit together. But the knowledge thus acquired will be misdirected unless we use it to enhance not lessen our sensitiveness to what is both actually and potentially novel and unique in our times. What Lawrence Frank remarks of Plato and Aristotle may be said of the authors of the great tradition whom Walter Lippmann wishes to give form and substance to the minds of the younger generation. "The persistent perplexities and aspirations of human life," says Frank, "that were familiar to them now confront us, and we must not evade our responsibilities by a nostalgic return to their formulations and procedures. As Santayana once remarked, 'a passion for the primitive is a sign of archaism in morals'; and, he might have added, a regression of intelligence."[10]

We want no regression of intelligence in education under the guise of a return to intellectual thoroughness.

And, finally, the school and the college in the post-war world, for which we must now plan, must give consideration to areas of experience totally neglected in the program of "Education for Freedom." We have in mind, for example, work experience such as the National Youth Administration used to such good purpose in vocational guidance and a number of schools and colleges are now employing as a maturing and stabilizing experience in social-civic education. Similarly we may hope to recognize more fully than at present the values of aesthetic and artistic development not merely for their indispensable contributions to personal growth but as one means of widening sympathy and enhancing the capacity to enter appreciatively into the lives of others.

[10] See "General Education," *The Social Frontier*, March and April, 1937.

The good school will thus strive to educate boys and girls healthy in body and spirit, keen in mind and deft of hand. Loyal to their tradition, yes. But so loyal that they do not hesitate, when need be, to preserve its essence by changing its outer forms and the institutions that serve as its medium in the image of a better tomorrow.

CHAPTER V

Education as Adjustment versus
Education to Meet the Needs of Youth

In contrast with the view that schools should concentrate primarily upon intellectual training is that of scientific education. This is specific and practical in its emphasis. It reduces all education to habit formation and quotes the psychology of behaviorism to deny originality in human beings. It reflects the machine character of our civilization and the depersonalizing effects of industrial and urban living. Education thus becomes at best high grade animal training. The child or youth is envisaged as being solely at the receiving end of the educational process. Accordingly he is to absorb the essential facts and principles already salted down within the major fields of learning; to make a part of himself acceptable codes of conduct; and to acquire those skills and techniques essential for successful performance in the workaday world.

Do you ask for criteria to employ in selecting what are at best a limited number of specifics out of literally hundreds of possibilities? Then are you referred to statistics, for it is statistics that enable us to choose from the stream of events those items which in turn may determine the nature of this stream. Values, desirable ways of living, of thinking, of believing are discoverable by statistics. Thus it is we arrive at the operations most appropriate to include in elementary arithmetic, or the facts to comprise a college survey course, or the skills indispensable to a vocational curriculum. Thus, too, do we identify the subjects to eliminate from school as well as new courses to introduce. An inspection of the presence or absence of the material in question within the activities of adults reveals its appropriateness for the indoctrination of children. And since values and ideals, on this theory, are reducible to the specific activities which identify them as such (courtesy, for example, with the actual performance of tipping the hat when meeting a lady, bowing on the customary occasion, and so on through an exhaustive list of occasions calling for courteous performances) education reduces to little more than the absorption of vast hordes of specific skills and abilities that young people will employ in the infinite number of concrete occasions of life. As one of the most enthusiastic advocates of this conception states,

The central theory is simple. Human life, however varied, consists in the performance of specific activities. Education that prepares for life is one that prepares definitely and adequately for these specific activities. However numerous and diverse they may be for any social class, they can be discovered. This requires only that one go out into the world of affairs and discover the particulars of which these affairs consist. These will show the abilities, attitudes, habits and appreciations and forms of knowledge that men need. These will be the objectives of the cirriculum. . . . The curriculum will then be that series of experiences which children and youth must have by way of attaining these objectives.[1]

The excesses of this school, as manifested in much of contemporary education, have quite properly elicited the scathing criticisms of President Hutchins as they did those of Abraham Flexner and others before him. In the name of science all sense of proportion and of values seem to disappear. For a time there was imminent danger that this "scientific" movement would give shape to the curriculum of the elementary and the secondary school. For example, elaborate studies were made of contemporary newspapers and magazines, under the auspices of well known educators, with a

[1] Franklin Bobbitt, *Curriculum Investigations*, p. 41. Boston: Houghton Mifflin Co., 1918.

view to determining quantitatively the facts of history to be taught. It was assumed that frequency of mention would constitute an objective criterion for the selection of historical events and personages to emphasize in contrast with the subjective judgments of mere historians! Similarly studies were made of items in science frequently mentioned in popular publications and from these data courses of study were constructed, designed to stress and to give information on these "most important" topics.

Fortunately the encroachments of this movement were checked on the elementary school level by the progressive education movement which had the merit of encouraging educators to observe actual children and their possibilities for growth.

II

On the higher levels of education the influence of scientific education is still strong. This explains the job analysis approach to trade education in secondary schools, and the attempt of many schools and the colleges alike to mould the ideas and the behavior of their students in harmony with the dominant religious, political and economic forces within the environment.

May we examine briefly the operations of this point of view as it affects education on the secondary and junior college levels.

First we should note that the ambitions of young people as well as the needs of the country have given a new, but, let us hope, a temporary impetus to vocational education of a narrow and specific character. Young people are once more in demand in industry, thus reversing an occupational trend characteristic of the decade preceding the war. Adult life, in the form of specialized and technical skills, once more beckons urgently to both boys and girls of adolescent age.

The war emergency necessitates that secondary schools respond to this demand. Accordingly, many schools are now offering pre-employment courses which train boys and girls (and girls increasingly) as well as adults, for specialized work in defense industries. Laudable, nay essential, as these courses are, unless they are cautiously administered and carefully related to the curriculum as a whole, they may involve us in the dangers of a penny-wise and pound-foolish policy. Unless they are supplemented and enriched by carefully planned experiences in general education and more general vocational preparation as well as by opportunities for retraining following the war, tragic outcomes may eventuate. The dangers involved in a too hasty preparation of our 'teen age youth for highly specialized operations in defense industries must be foreseen and carefully guarded against lest, in the process of winning the war, we sow the seeds for a harvest of disillusioned unemployables in the post-war world.

Unless the war reverses long time trends in business and industry neither highly specialized training nor preparation as such for entrance into trades and vocations prior to the junior college period will constitute a wise education for the run of the mine of American youth.

Studies of the American Youth Commission prior to the war indicated a steady trend on the part of business and industry toward the exclusion of young people from participation in economic life under the age of twenty. In view of these trends the Commission recommended raising the school-leaving age and the postponement of vocational education until at least the upper years of the high school and the junior college.

Moreover, even at this point, the evidence runs counter to overly specific vocational training until relatively late in the school curriculum. Far better is a division of labor between agencies out-of-school and the school system that permits the school to center upon general education, and business and industry to give specific training on-the-job. Dr. Homer Rainey writes in this connection:

The high schools should concentrate their vocational training upon a program of generalized vocational education which would be applicable to a family of occupations. Studies now being made by the United States Employment Service are beginning to reveal large possibilities of classification of jobs into closely related families in the sense that they require a similar type of training. Studies also indicate that by far the vast majority of this training can be done in short-term courses ranging from three weeks to six months, and that this training is best done in close relation to the job.[2]

Dr. Rainey likewise advocates a close interrelationship between vocational and liberal education. Thus he writes:

When the vocational outlooks open to young people are analyzed, it becomes evident that groups of courses can be arranged, each group having certain common elements. For example, all the vocations which deal with machinery have a common background in physical science. All the vocations which are of the type commonly classified as commercial have a background in economics. The learned professions have a background in history and literature.

The relation between the liberal and the vocational parts of the secondary-school curriculum has been a subject of violent controversy in recent years. The time has come when this controversy must end if young people are to have proper preparation for life. A plan of instruction must be adopted which will include for all pupils both vocational education and general, or liberal, education in the true sense of the word. The two kinds of education are not antithetical but supplementary. . . . How long the vocational curriculum is to keep any given pupil in school will be determined largely by the exactions of the vocation chosen. Whatever the period of schooling, the school should at all times aim to cultivate two types of intellectual maturity, two types of information, and two types of interpretation of the facts known to modern science and letters—one vocational in its interests and applications; one general, directly related to the common social life of humanity.[3]

[2] "The Needs of American Youth: What the American Youth Commission Has Found." *Practical Values of Educational Research* (Washington, D. C., American Research Association, 1938), p. 177.

[3] Homer P. Rainey and others, *How Fare American Youth?* pp. 56–57. New York: D. Appleton-Century Co., 1937.

The junior college has assumed in recent years the position occupied by the junior high school some thirty years ago. At that time it was assumed that the large mass of students would terminate their education at the conclusion of the junior high school period and would thus be equipped with both a general education and some vocational skill of a specific character. Today it is the junior college that is envisaged as a terminal educational institution. The directors of these schools have been impressed with the facts of unemployment of youth between the ages of sixteen and twenty. They recognize the social necessity that schooling be substituted for idleness and they conclude with Doak S. Campbell that education for this hundred per cent must be designed "to achieve broad social ends, of which preparation for scholarly pursuits is but a part."[4]

When this situation faced educators some years ago, on the upper elementary and junior high school levels, the answer was uniformity, standardization, and the organization of what William Heard Kilpatrick has called "pre-digested subject matter." It is not surprising, therefore, to find a similar tendency operating where mass education has moved up a rung or two on the educational ladder.

Vocational courses have thus established themselves in junior colleges and in the lower divisions of universities as well as in the first two years of many liberal arts colleges. These vocational courses, moreover, operate in large measure on the assumption that vocational preparation should be of a specific character leading to the acquisition of specific skills and operations.

One of the most influential leaders in this movement was the late Robert J. Leonard, one-time director of vocational education at the University of California. Leonard accumulated evidence to indicate three tendencies in industry, business, and the professions. First is an upgrading of occupations,

---

[4] *Thirty-Eighth Yearbook*, National Society for the Study of Education, Part II, p. 116.

a tendency for types of work that were once rudimentary and simple to develop into practices that are scientific and involved and require careful training for their performance. Thus the contractor becomes an engineer and the domestic servant who cares for the sick a trained nurse. Secondly, professions that were once wholes have become subdivided into parts which in many cases are as extensive as the original profession. Dentistry, for example, includes not only the dentist, orthodentist and research dentist but the dental nurse, the dental hygienist, the dental mechanic. And third, Leonard observes, it is less customary than formerly for individuals to pass from one level to a higher occupational level. A competent dental mechanic may receive additional salary, or, perhaps be promoted to more responsible work in his field, but he remains a mechanic, he does not become a dentist.

In this connection, Leonard remarked:

> Some friends of liberty who speak and write much of democracy and American institutions deplore this situation; they wish it were different; they would legislate if they could. But they deplore it because they have only partial knowledge of the whole situation. They entirely fail to grasp the significance of the fact that within each level there are now wider ranges for service, promotion and salary than in former days when occupations were complete entities.[5]

This emphasis upon specific training of a job analysis character has decided educational and practical limitations.

On the practical side it involves the danger that semi-professional training will do no more than many trade courses; namely, equip the student for what may prove to be a blind alley performance. By concentrating upon specific education the student fails to secure a fundamental training in general principles which cut through a variety of specific operations and thus enable him later to adjust to the changes

[5] "Professional Education in Junior Colleges," *Teachers College Record*, Vol. XXVI, May, 1925, p. 729.

and transformations that inevitably occur in these specific operations.

Nor is industry altogether satisfied with vocational education based upon a job analysis, for the reason that skills thus taught tend to lag behind business and industrial practice. It would seem, then, that institutions which seek to crowd into a course of one or two years all possible training in the acquisition of technical skills, with a consequent neglect of cultural and general education, fail to meet both the obligations of a public education and the requirements of a vocation.

They fail to meet the obligations of a public education in two respects.

In the first place they deny to many students an open door to opportunity. To assume with Leonard that because promotions from one level of occupations to a higher are less frequent than formerly, the school should organize its work with a view to confirming this state of affairs is indeed to train for the status quo. It would transform an uncontrolled economic trend into a fixed order. Moreover, if schools adopt this policy they will place obstacles in the form of overly specialized and narrow curricula in the way of all students who possess the ability to advance, let us say, from the position of pharmacist to a biochemist, but who are economically incapable of doing so at once. Specific job training, in practice, results in subjecting students to specific courses relating only to occupations on one level of performance and denying to them an access to foundational and general training courses that have a leading-on value.

Vocational curricula consisting of courses directed exclusively toward specific vocational ends neglect the obvious fact that a student who enters a vocation must function as a citizen, as a member of a family and in a host of relationships other than vocational, which bear vitally upon the public welfare.

While a worker may exercise a number of functions in society which are unrelated to his particular vocation, others will grow naturally out of it. More and more, for example, individuals tend to exercise citizenship functions through vocational groups. Indeed one of the characteristics of American life in recent years is the development of vocational organizations that provide opportunities for their members both to continue their technical training and to engage in activities that involve their relation to the public in general. So, too, there is a growing tendency for functional organizations to deal directly with government on matters of legislation affecting their interests and to concern themselves with problems affecting the public interest. The activities of these groups can be self-seeking and self-centered. This follows when a vocation is sensed exclusively in its economic context. On the other hand, if vocational education includes a history and a civics specifically designed to help young people sense their vocational ancestry, and to acquire an understanding and appreciation of the far-reaching social significance of their vocational activities, quite different results may follow. A vocational social science of this character will go far toward enabling a worker to sense directly the social implications of his work and thus offset what John Dewey believes to be one of the most serious aspects of modern life: the growing inability of the individual to trace vital lines of connection between his vocational activity and its social effects.

III

It would not be accurate to convey the impression that a conception of education which is primarily concerned with adjustment operates solely in public junior colleges or in the field of vocational education. It influences as well the curricula of a goodly number of colleges and universities which have organized their first two years in lower divisions or junior colleges, and it characterizes much of the experimentation in private as well as public two-year junior colleges.

Take, for example, survey courses as commonly organized. These courses evolve out of the legitimate desire to read unity and consistency of pattern into the student's education, to give him an overview of representative fields of knowledge, or an equally complete introduction to the facts and principles and activities within a functional area of living. As an introduction to fields of knowledge this movement probably reached its culminating point some years ago at Colgate University, where students in their freshman year were required to devote two-thirds of their time to five survey courses; surveys of the physical sciences, the biological sciences, the social sciences, the fine arts, philosophy and religion. Of these courses President Cutten wrote:

> Colgate is aware that it did not invent the survey course, but it believes it is the first to carry the idea to its logical conclusion, and that its five courses spreading over the whole domain of human knowledge, and required of all freshmen, constitute a departure in college education.[6]

While other colleges of liberal arts and junior colleges have been less ambitious as regards the program of a student in a single year, survey courses designed to help him "master the leading ideas and significant facts in the principal fields of knowledge" as intended at the University of Chicago, for example, are on the increase.

Survey courses are not confined, however, to overviews of representative fields of knowledge. Of recent years attempts have been made to use them as introductions to functional areas of living. Thus Stephens College, Missouri, has pioneered in a new type of organization. Under the direction of W. W. Charters a survey was made of the activities in

[6] Quoted from the Survey by the American Association of University Women. *Thirty-First Yearbook*, National Society for the Study of Education, Part II, pp. 46–47.

which women actually engage, the problems and the needs they encounter in the course of their daily lives. These returns were classified into seven areas[7] of activity, and problems and courses were designed to enable the students of Stephens to acquire the principles and facts and skills essential to function adequately as women.

Some years ago Goucher College also engaged in an interesting attempt to make education functional. Taking its cue from the procedure of the United States Department of State in establishing standards of eligibility for departmental posts by analyzing "records of usage" which reveal the duties actually performed by the office in question, the college attempted to determine "what qualifications, preparation, and training would be useful to a Goucher graduate in living her life." Eight objectives of general education[8] were formulated which the college believed to relate directly to the life activities of women. While courses were organized to realize these objectives no course other than English constituted an absolute requirement. On the contrary, the student's progress was appraised in terms of progress toward the objectives, and her courses selected with these ends in mind.

This basic approach in the selection of subject matter or activities, is not unlike the method of job analysis as applied in vocational and semi-professional education. Emphasis is not upon the student, his interests or the peculiarities of his situation as such but rather upon what should be inculcated

[7] These areas are: communications, physical health, mental health, aesthetics, social adjustment, economics, religion.

[8] These objectives are:
  (1) to establish and maintain physical and mental health;
  (2) to comprehend and communicate ideas both in English and in foreign languages;
  (3) to understand the scientific method in theory and application;
  (4) to understand the heritage of the past in its relation to the present;
  (5) to establish satisfying relations with individuals and with groups;
  (6) to utilize resources with economic and aesthetic satisfaction;
  (7) to enjoy literature and the other arts;
  (8) to appreciate religious and philosophical values.

in him. The organizers of survey courses resort to diverse methods in determining the facts and principles to be taught. The crudest device consists in balancing the interests of related departments which are often competitors for the future allegiance of students. A second employs statistical and scientific methods for arriving at a concensus of judgments of authorities in the fields represented. Still a third utilizes the results of an activity or functional analysis similar to that of Charters at Stephens College.

But how does this differ essentially from the procedure used in organizing a vocational course in which the existing state of a vocation is accepted as a standard, its processes analyzed, and students prepared specifically in the performance of those operations as revealed by the job analysis? The psychological assumptions would seem to be similar. In each case the learner is primarily a recipient. He is either a mind to absorb what is presented to him or an organism to be conditioned to think and to feel and to act in predetermined ways. This trend in general education leans heavily upon behavioristic and mechanistic psychology and the statistical and scientific tools which its devotees employ for selecting from the inexhaustible resources of knowledge or the multiplicity of activities of men those which quantitatively and objectively viewed seem to be of most importance.

IV

The same practical concerns that eventuated in educational programs based upon careful surveys of cultural needs and resources, of books and of life, has led to provision for the guidance of students. The guidance movement grew out of a common-sense emphasis upon the importance of helping students to fit into the requirements of school and college life, to cope effectively with the curriculum, to meet the demands of social adjustment and of social living. It recognized that individuals differ in their interests and their abilities and it proposed that assistance be rendered students in meeting the educational requirements common to all.

But the guidance movement also implied a respect for individual differences. It accepted the fact that differences in interests and abilities and in life goals are legitimate concerns of a democratic education. Consequently to the emphasis which guidance took over from business and industrial management (an objective appraisal of the students' assets and liabilities as a first condition for fitting him nicely into educational grooves) was added a respect for the peculiarities of the individual personality. As the sources of these peculiarities have been studied and the origin of the problems and the concerns, as well as the maladjustments of students have become better known, educators have acquired an insight into student development that bids fair to transform earlier and more limited conceptions of the "needs" of individuals and of society alike. What began as an attempt the better to adjust students to school and to life has become a significant effort to reorganize the purposes and the materials of general education. In many institutions of school and college grade this movement has led to a thoroughgoing revision of the curriculum in the light of student needs. Moreover the concept of a need as a basis for educational planning is undergoing change. The concerns, the problems, the interests of an individual are viewed as the unique expression within him of the events and the forces of the cultural medium of which he is a part. Conversely the needs or demands of society, as the educator encounters and uses them are but partial descriptions, abstractions, of desirable characteristics of the culture—its traditions, expectations, pressures, longed-for relationships and arrangements of its people which can find reality only in the lives and activities of concrete personalities. These demands are met in a healthy manner only when they complement, reinforce and fuse healthily with the living tissues of personalities. The needs of society and the individual are thus but two sides of one and the same shield. Accordingly there has developed still a third trend in general education commonly called the "needs approach." It is an attempt to identify the points of growing pain alike in the individual and the society which sustains him, to determine what are the general problems of growth, of concern and of interest for the student, to ascertain what in his culture gives rise to these problems; and by means of analysis and study of concrete individuals in specific situations to provide those resources of material and experience which will enable the student creatively to meet his needs in working harmony with the major values of a democratic society.

Reference has been made to the functional courses at Stephens College and the functional objectives of Goucher College. It is therefore necessary to draw attention to the careful provisions for personal guidance of students at each of these institutions. At Stephens an advisory system exists which associates each teacher intimately with ten students.[9] The advisor encourages his students to study their own needs, to select their own goals of effort, to evaluate their progress and to participate in appropriate activities. In addition there are counselors or clinicians to give specialized assistance to students on the advisor's recommendations. Assignments within courses are differentiated and often the content modified with respect to the interests and needs of students thus determined. So, too, at Goucher the realization of the objectives of general education are sought both through the guidance which advisors can give and by means of a flexible arrangement of schedules and programs.

The work of the General College at the University of Minnesota also illustrates this new trend. Here, under the leadership of former Dean MacLean, a thorough study was made of all who enrolled in the general college, their backgrounds, their interests, their attitudes, their abilities, and the circumstances and conditions of their life at home and

[9] See B. Lamar Johnson, *Thirty-Eighth Yearbook*, National Society for the Study of Education, Part II, pp. 128–134; also "A Woman's Right to a Right Education" by James Madison Wood in *Progressive Education*, Vol. XV, January, 1939, pp. 44–50.

in the college, all with the purpose of securing an accurate and intimate picture of the student and his needs. Secondly, the General College studied groups of young adults who had recently left the University. This study, writes MacLean,

covered pertinent questions on four areas of adult activity and interests: (1) earning a living, (2) home and family life, (3) personal life, (4) social and civic life. Within each of these areas we set up batteries of questions probing for the problems, activities, and interests of the adults involved.[10]

On the basis of these findings the General College replaced ten of its earlier survey courses with courses designed to help students deal constructively with their needs in four major areas. These courses were Personal Life Orientation, Home and Family-Life Orientation, General Vocational Orientation, Social and Civic Orientation.

It is interesting to observe that the four areas of student needs identified at the University of Minnesota correspond with classifications of needs that have emerged from investigations elsewhere. For example, the Adolescent Study of the Commission on the Secondary School Curriculum of the Progressive Education Association accumulated case study data on some six hundred fifty young people. Most of these young people were enrolled in secondary schools and colleges. Some were being assisted by the National Youth Administration. Some were in a vocational school. Their needs fell into categories practically identical with those of the Minnesota study. Moreover, schools and colleges which work intimately with relatively small groups of students seem to discover similar classifications.

We might enumerate other studies of young people's needs in order to sustain the substantial validity of those already mentioned. However, the essential point is the fact that many educators in schools and colleges alike are attempting to determine from studies of groups of individuals and from

[10] *Thirty-Eighth Yearbook,* National Society for the Study of Education, Part II, p. 145.

intensive individual case studies what are the actual needs of young people and how these needs take character from the peculiar circumstances surrounding the individual (political, social, economic); and, on the basis of their findings, are seeking to organize and reorganize the curriculum of secondary school and college. As Powers, Bigelow, MacLean and others have shown in the Thirty-Eighth Yearbook of the National Society for the Study of Education, determined efforts are now under way to provide materials of instruction capable of adaptation to varied types of curricula organization in harmony with this general trend. Likewise the reports of the Commission on the Secondary School Curriculum of the Progressive Education Association contain recommendations along these lines for the major fields of secondary education.

The attempt to make available material and resources for general education appropriate to the needs of young people may resemble at times the ancient tendency to pour old wine into new bottles. But this is not entirely the case. For one thing, it seeks to utilize the first-hand experience of young people in a manner "Education for Freedom" would eschew. Similarly it differs from the methods and the ends of the job analysis. For example, as against specific vocational training in general education this third group would involve young people in significant adult activities because of the basic educational values thus realized. These experiences may serve incidentally the purposes of general vocational orientation, but, over and above these outcomes, it is sought to give young people a sense of performing a task that is socially significant, of thus revealing the full meaning of principles encountered in classroom or laboratory, or, as in the case of routine work experience, the social and cultural as well as the economic possibilities of work. As Bigelow and MacLean remark,

More and more institutions concerned with general education are sending their students out into the market places, into the legislatures, into the art studios, into the factories that produce power and goods of every sort, out to see the farms, the railroads and other agencies of communication.[11]

Antioch, Bennington, Sarah Lawrence, and other colleges have observed the maturing effects of work as an inherent part of the college program. Similarly some of the National Youth Encampments prior to their abandonment, the Volunteer Service Camps of the Friends' Service Committee, and the camps of The Associated Junior Work Camps, Inc. are revealing hitherto untapped possibilities for vitalizing principles in the natural and social sciences, as well as affording concrete opportunities for young people to meet certain essential needs by engaging in socially significant enterprises.

Careful scrutiny of these tendencies reveals still a further characteristic, one that sets it off clearly from the program of Hutchins and Barr and Van Doren. It is an attempt to acquaint young people with what Lawrence K. Frank describes as "the emerging new ideas and conceptions, already implicit in our sciences and arts today, that are to dominate our future culture." The formalist would use the old books as a means for helping young people to find the answers to "the eternal problems which their ancestors faced before them and which recur with each generation." The newer point of view would use some of these books in order better to understand the origin and the history of present problems. At the same time it recognizes that problems today are unique and thus require unique answers.

In the previous chapter, and in this, we have endeavored to outline briefly three major trends in general education. These three relatively distinct philosophies and programs are evident in the curricula of our schools and colleges. Few institutions, however, will serve as clean-cut illustrations of any one. A visitor from abroad is more likely to encounter confusion and contradiction. Even where administration and faculty are committed in their hearts to the realization of a

[11] "Dominant Trends in General Education," *General Education in the American College*, Thirty-Eighth Yearbook, National Society for the Study of Education, Part II, p. 366.

common philosophy, compromise and adjustment to practical situations often eventuate in inconsistent practices.

Furthermore there are lines of general agreement as between these trends which on occasion disguise more basic conflicts. For example, all are responsive to the fact that general education must serve a more widely selected group than heretofore. Indeed it is commonly recognized that educational plans and programs must be planned with an eye to the educational requirements of all youth between the ages of sixteen and twenty. Secondly, each seeks a substitute for the elective system which has pulverized the educational experiences of young people. Each agrees that greater unity and integration must be introduced into the student's education. And, finally, through the organization of courses and through personnel or guidance work there is fairly general recognition that young people must be assisted in reading purpose and meaning into their lives.

These are significant agreements. But the disagreements are also significant; perhaps crucial for the future of American democracy. Consequently it is essential that they not be glossed over. It is not a matter of indifference to American youth or to American society where young people will go in order to find the answers to the problems they believe are most vital to their welfare and their future. Nor is it of little consequence whether we conceive of learning as essentially an absorptive process, or as habit formation, or as the discovery of truths that exist without reference to the changing circumstances of men, or as a creative process in which a unique self now wrestles with its environment, now cooperates with its surroundings in an effort to produce a manner of living that is genuinely novel. Theories of learning are in the end identical with what their advocates believe to be the nature of man and of the good society. The issues of education are indeed the issues of life; and what each of us believes should characterize general education is one with what he hopes in fact will become the world of tomorrow.

CHAPTER VI

Religion and the Public Schools

THE issue of church and state, long dormant in American life, is coming to the fore again. For the depression and the war have brought a steady and accelerating growth of religious instruction in our public schools, and this new trend brings into conflict large bodies of earnest people who want it to go still further, and other citizens who fear that it will foster division and disunity in a population as varied in creed and background as ours.

Various methods of introducing religious education into the public schools are already employed. In some communities, predominantly of one denomination or one faith, the churches and the public schools join in selecting religious teachers who thereupon conduct regularly scheduled classes on school time and often in the school building. In other communities religious education is recognized as a normal function of the regular teacher. For example, a city school system in the South reports as follows:

Assembly is held three times a week, opened with Bible reading and prayer; usually the Lord's Prayer is repeated in concert. For variety Bible verses are memorized and repeated in concert. Once a year the minister of each denomination is asked to speak at assembly period. Each Monday the childern are asked if they attended any Sunday School or church the preceding Sunday. A record is kept.

Still a third method is more sensitive to the American conception of the separation of church and state. This is the method of "released time." For example, in a number of states, children of parents who request it are excused from school at a given hour once a week to attend religious classes in church schools. Probably a thousand or more communities in the United States have in operation plans of this sort.

On the surface the method of released time seems to avoid the constitutional difficulties that have prevented school officials and church authorities from joining forces for the religious education of children. Nevertheless in ten states (California, Iowa, Kentucky, Maine, Massachusetts, Minnesota, New York, Oregon, South Dakota, and West Virginia) it has seemed essential for the legislatures to approve specifically a released-time program. Elsewhere such programs have relied upon decisions rendered by school officials, in accordance with the general provisions of the law, or on rulings of state attorneys general. (The rulings have been by no means unanimous: in eight states the attorneys general and court decisions have authorized the release of pupils from school for religious instruction, while in three states the attorneys general have ruled against it.)

If we are to understand the nature and significance of this re-emerging issue we must look into its background.

First we should remind ourselves that public schools represent a relatively late development in our educational history. American schools originated as sectarian, religious institutions. Not until roughly 1830, in the period of Jacksonian democracy, did public education at public expense become an accepted policy; and not until the court decision in the famous Kalamazoo case in Michigan, in 1874, was it clearly established that taxes might be levied in support of public high schools as well as public elementary schools.

It was natural that the states, in providing for public education, should insist upon the principle of separation of church and state; for this principle was commonly embodied in state constitutions and had become generally accepted as a cardinal principle of American life. It had not been abruptly arrived at. The first settlements in America had been religious settlements undertaken by people who wanted to worship God according to the dictates of their own conscience. Only gradually did they come to see that the right they claimed for themselves was a duty they owed to others. The governments that they set up were originally Congregational in Massachusetts, Anglican in Virginia, Catholic in Maryland. But new settlements brought new religious sects, religious tension increased, and only the tolerance and the foresight of men like William Penn in Pennsylvania, and the practical need for finding ways in which diverse groups could live together with some semblance of harmony in a polyglot religious community, gave birth to the concept of religious freedom. In order to insure this freedom the colonies and later the states gradually adopted the policy of benevolent neutrality toward all religious groups and special favors toward none —the policy that we characterize as the separation of church and state.

Naturally the schools reflected this development. They, too, began as narrow sectarian institutions, designed to instruct young people in the tenets of the true faith and to breed fear and hostility toward unbelief and unbelievers. But denominational schools were difficult to finance, so gradually they opened their doors to children of various other Protestant sects, and accordingly the instruction tended to become less sectarian. By 1830, when Jacksonian democracy gave impetus to the development of public schools, publicly supported, the principle of nonsectarian instruction was already fairly well established.

From nonsectarian instruction the next step was to secular instruction. The change came slowly, but by the beginning of the present century a combination of factors had succeeded in altogether eliminating religious instruction from the public schools in most of our states. These factors were (1) the objections registered by Jews, Catholics, and non-

believers to "nonsectarian" instruction that was essentially
Protestant in character; (2) a belated recognition on the part
of liberal religious groups that the forcing of religious doctrines upon children of alien mind was an ineffective method
of promoting these doctrines; and (3) the widespread secu-
larizing influences in American life that tended to divert
men's minds from religious preoccupations.

During the period from 1830 to the present the tide of
court decisions on this question has ebbed and flowed. While
the constitutions of many states forbade religious instruction
in public schools, common practice and court decisions were
slow to interpret these prohibitions as applying to the reading
of the Bible or the repeating of the Lord's Prayer. For example, a Maine court in 1854 sustained the expulsion of a
Catholic child from school because of his refusal to read
from a Protestant Bible; and both a Kansas and a Texas court,
in 1904 and 1906 respectively, refused to consider the reading of the Bible and the use of the Lord's Prayer as running
counter to the Constitution or to statutes prohibiting religious
worship and sectarian instruction in the schoolroom. An
annotation of the Wisconsin Statutes of 1898 was typical of
a general atmosphere in which non-Protestant, agnostic, and
atheistic groups fared badly. It stated that Constitutional
prohibitions against sectarian teaching referred exclusively
"to religious doctrines which are believed by some religious
sects and rejected by others," but that "to teach the existence
of a supreme being of infinite wisdom, power, and goodness,
and that it is the duty of all men to adore, obey, and love
him, is not sectarian because all religious . . . sects so believe
and teach."

On the other hand, there was a steady drift toward secular
instruction during the last quarter of the last century and the
first quarter of the present one. In 1872 the Board of Education of Cincinnati forbade the reading of the Bible in public
schools. In 1890 the Supreme Court of Wisconsin held that
the reading of the Bible was unconstitutional on the ground

that it constituted sectarian instruction. In 1902, 1910, and 1915 respectively the Supreme Courts of Nebraska, Illinois, and Louisiana rendered similar decisions. Soon other states began to follow suit in practice if not in law. As Howard K. Beale points out in his *History of Freedom of Teaching in American Schools*,[1] liberal groups, including liberal Protestant ministers, united in the 1870's with Catholics and Jews as well as agnostics in a campaign for public schools that would be truly free of religion. Gradually these efforts bore fruit; whereas, for example, as late as 1903 ten states still required the reading of the Bible in the schools, by 1913 only two insisted upon it.

Naturally this trend was affected by the arrival in America of great numbers of immigrants with new and strange religious views. In many localities these immigrants were greeted with suspicion and fear; hence the insistence of many of the older American groups upon defining nonsectarian instruction in Protestant terms. On the other hand, the objection of Catholics and Jews as well as liberals to defining nonsectarian instruction in Protestant terms appealed to fair-minded people and gave impetus to the exclusion of all religious teaching from the schools. Gradually many came to believe that a principle which barred the teaching of material in dispute between Protestant sects should also bar the teaching of material in dispute as between Protestants, Jews, Catholics, and even nonbelievers.

The same motive of fair play to Catholics, Jews, and others led gradually also to the provision that no public funds should be used to support denominational or private schools. In 1875 President Grant suggested the adoption of a constitutional amendment that would forbid the teaching of religious tenets and prohibit "the granting of any school funds or school taxes . . . either by legislative, municipal, or other authority, for the benefit or in aid, directly or indirectly, of any religious sect or denomination." The purpose of advo-

[1] Published by Charles Scribner's Sons, 1941.

cates of strict neutrality was not antireligious; Grant and others were equally insistent that the Constitution be altered, if necessary, in order to insure that the schools be safeguarded from "pagan" and "atheistic" tenets. But some of these advocates were animated by an impulse less generous than that of fair play: they wanted to exclude Catholic and other "foreign" sects from the benefits of public support. As a result of this mixture of motives, laws were enacted and clauses written into state constitutions prohibiting the use of public moneys on behalf of sectarian schools. By 1903 state aid for religious schools was forbidden in thirty-nine states.

It is interesting to observe the attitude of Catholics toward these developments. As Howard K. Beale indicates in the volume mentioned above, Catholics were torn between a desire to keep their children in parochial schools and a desire to free both Catholic children and Catholic teachers from the necessity of using the Protestant Bible in public school classes. Consequently, in the third quarter of the nineteenth century Catholics joined with Jews, freethinkers, and other dissidents in opposing the reading of the Bible and all compulsory nonsectarian religious instruction in the public schools, while at the same time they strove to secure public funds with which to develop parochial schools; and in cities where Catholics won political power they succeeded both in eliminating the Bible from the schools and in securing the employment of Catholic teachers.

On the whole Catholics have consistently maintained the position that the state should support denominational schools.[2] It is fairly generally accepted Catholic theory that schools should be administered by the churches and supported financially by the state. Thus at a meeting of the American Federation of Catholic Societies in 1906 the following declaration of policy was adopted:

[2] For an excellent discussion of both Catholic and Protestant parochial schools in American life, see Chapters V–VII of *Church and State: The American Way*, by Conrad Henry Moehlman, Harper & Brothers, New York, 1944.

First, let no public moneys be paid out for religious instruction in any school; secondly, let the educational per capita tax be distributed for results in purely secular studies only in our Catholic schools, our teachers receiving their salaries as other teachers receive theirs; thirdly, to obtain these results let our schools be submitted to state or city examinations.

Evidently this is still an accurate statement of Catholic policy and accounts for repeated efforts on the part of Catholics to secure financial assistance from state governments with which to ease the expense of maintaining parochial schools.

The attitude of orthodox Jewish groups toward the public schools is different. In general, they have united with opponents of religious instruction in the public schools because they considered this instruction biased. Consequently, they have preferred on the whole to use the weekday synagogue school for religious education as well as for instruction in the Jewish heritage. They have thus tended both to avoid the parochial school and to oppose the idea of a released-time program.

It is clear from all this that religious instruction has never been barred completely from the public schools in the United States. Nor is it wise to infer that it is any longer on the wane. Anti-evolution laws in Southern states represent one means for insuring a religious interpretation of the origin and nature of man. The prohibition against sectarian instruction, where this prohibition exists, is variously interpreted, meaning often in homogeneous communities merely the elimination of items upon which Protestant sects disagree. At the other extreme we can find school systems, particularly in heterogeneous communities, that interpret strictly the principle of separation of church and state. In these schools all mention of religion is carefully avoided, textbooks or discussions in history or the sciences that relate to controversial topics are carefully eliminated, and the suggestion that a program of released time be introduced is interpreted as a reversion to an unenlightened past.

II

How shall we explain the new trend toward religious instruction under public auspices?

The most potent factor is doubtless psychological: fear of impending change—change in manners and morals such as that which characterized the "revolt of youth" in recent years; fear of fundamental alterations under way in our economic life; fear of changes in government, particularly those threatened by foreign "isms" such as fascism and communism; fear on the part of organized religious groups that without state intervention large numbers of children will grow up strangers to religion.

Seldom do fears operate singly. Particularly are men adept at utilizing the fears of their neighbors in order to ward off threats against their own sacred preserves. Accordingly, economic conservatives see in religious instruction one means of teaching respect for traditional property rights; religious groups, fearful of the effect of science upon conventional religious ideas, and incidentally upon church membership, say that there is a necessary relationship between religious belief and adherence to the democratic form of government; and political conservatives, citing the attacks upon religion that followed the adoption of communism in Russia or national socialism in Germany, use religious orthodoxy as an instrument with which to ward off both political radicalism and political liberalism.

Nor should we lose sight of the traditional notion, so commonly accepted uncritically, that religious belief is essential for moral development.

A simple statement of this attitude appeared a few years ago in a letter to the *New York Times*, when the proposal for a released-time program was pending before the Board of Education. Said the letter:

A good Catholic can never be a bad citizen. Likewise neither can a good Protestant or a good Jew fail in ligation. If, as one authority has said, there are hundreds of thousands of "spiritually hungry and spiritually naked" children in New York City alone, then a challenge exists that must be met promptly and fully. These children, to be good citizens, are in desperate need of religious orientation.

A similar line of reasoning prompted the legislature of the state of Maine in 1939 to authorize provision for moral instruction of pupils in the public schools in accordance with their religious faith.

Naturally church authorities see certain practical advantages in tying religious education to the public schools. In the first place, it constitutes an easy and effective means for reaching the children of the unchurched as well as the churched. For example, W. Dyer Blair wrote in the *Church Monthly* of the Riverside Church of New York City for May, 1940, "Neither the Sunday, the vocation church school, nor the young people's societies, nor all three combined, reach as high as percentage of the total youth group in a great many communities as does the weekday church." And in the second place, weekday instruction enables religious groups to provide better-trained teachers and better teaching than was possible under the Sunday-school plan of volunteer instruction.

Recently an influential group of liberals in religion has brought forward a new argument against secular education. They say that it offends against the fundamental tenets of modern education by not meeting the needs of the whole child. Affirming a fundamental weakness in Western culture —that it is shallow and superficial, lacking an integrating spiritual principle—these liberals argue that we need to provide a more adequate framework of values for men to hold in common.

These people also contend that the present secular character of education tends to perpetuate the weakness and superficiality of our culture by setting religion apart from of life. This group, in the words of Professor F.

Ernest Johnson of Columbia University, would like "to see the same attention given to the religious life of the community as is given in the social studies to business, politics, art, and public welfare." If the curriculum is to be built around "life experiences," they say, how absurd to leave out religion, as if it didn't rate inclusion![3]

When we ask ourselves precisely what sort of ultimate program these people wish we do not receive an altogether clear answer. Obviously they would like the schools to be more willing to introduce *knowledge about* religion: to include comparative religion on the higher levels, to refrain from excluding material touching upon religion and religious institutions in history and the social studies, and certainly to inform children about the religious life and religious groups within their own communities—all as an inherent part of the school curriculum. But evidently this is only one step in the total program suggested. Professor F. Ernest Johnson, for example, writing in the *Information Service* of the Federal Council of the Churches of Christ in America, distinguishes sharply between sectarian and religious education, arguing that state laws exclude the former and not the latter from the schools. Religious education, he holds, does not consist of doctrines which divide religious groups from each other, nor does it include necessarily specific doctrines. Religion concerns itself rather with those "assumptions concerning the good life which hold society together; with belief in the value of reverence and in the importance of belonging to a worshiping, working, religious community; with devotion to the ends that find their meaning outside the scope and span of the individual life—in short . . . spiritual values that make for the untiy of a dynamic culture." Consequently, he argues, religion should assume a central role in the education of every child.

[3] For a recent statement of this position, see *Church and State in Education*, by William Clayton Bowers, University of Chicago Press, Chicago, Ill., 1944.

It is obvious, of course, that religious education of this character cannot be provided for adequately by released time. Indeed, Harrison Elliott and other religious educators, who view religion as a community experience, criticize the plan for released time precisely *because* it constitutes a divisive element in the child's experience and introduces still another atomistic element into the already broken-up experiences of children. "Children," says Mr. Elliott, "are nurtured in Christian life and experience, not by knowledge of the Bible or the creeds of the church per se, but through their choices and their experiences in home and school and community." Consequently, Mr. Elliott departs from the proposals of many of his colleagues in religious education and urges (1) that provision be made for dismsised time for which the school is in no way responsible; and (2) that within this time (considerably more than one hour per week) the churches should organize an adequate program that involves children within the life of a church community.

III

Will religious education under public auspices realize these worthy aims? There is little in our past to sustain such a hope.

Indeed there is grave danger that the opposite will be true: that a revival of religious instruction within the schoolroom —or under conditions that require school officials to check and control attendance upon religious centers—will keep alive or fan into flame old religious and racial animosities. Certainly in the past the unfortunate tendency on the part of many zealots to identify morality with conformity to their own religious presuppositions has by no means fostered "assumptions concerning the good life which hold society together." On the contrary, as Charles and Mary Beard have pointed out in *The Rise of American Civilization*, it was the bickering and rivalry between religious sects that constituted one of the original motives for the establishment of secular schools.

Since those days our public education may have failed in many respects, but one thing it has done. It has contributed much toward unifying children of diverse racial, national, and religious origins. In recent years, serious fissures have occurred in American life. There has been an insidious growth of anti-Semitism. Conflicts between blacks and whites have flared into race riots. Intolerance of minorities has been widespread. Our American unity is sorely tried. Is it not an unfortunate time in which to use the school as an instrument for calling attention to the differences between children of Catholic, Protestant, and Jewish faith?

And what of the rights of the child who falls outside these conventional groupings? Many parents have severed their church connections or retain only a technical church membership. They wish to postpone, if not to eliminate, the religious issue for their children. These unchurched parents are required to face an unfair dilemma. Shall they expose their children to the charge of being "queer" or "godless," or shall they conform and insist that their children receive instruction in a context to which they object?

Nor is this danger confined exclusively to the unchurched. It applies wherever a child belongs to a conspicuous minority. In overwhelmingly Catholic sections the finger of deviation will point to the Protestant. In a Protestant locality all non-Protestants will be identified as unbelievers. It requires little insight into the principles of mental hygiene to realize that this situation is charged with psychological as well as social danger.

It is commonly assumed by those who oppose our secular schools that religious instruction is a necessary condition for the moral education of children. But surely there is little evidence that moral fiber is dependent upon orthodoxy of any one kind. Who will contend, for example, that the principles we admire in an honest business man, an incorruptible judge, or a faithful public servant derive from convictions that mark him off as Baptist, Presbyterian, or Methodist, or as Catholic,

Protestant, Jew, or skeptic? Indeed, one could even argue that religious education as commonly provided has very little influence at all upon morality; witness these excerpts from a recent paper by Dr. Negley K. Teeters, Professor of Sociology at Temple University:

> Some years ago, Dr. George Rex Mursall, chief psychologist of the Ohio Department of Welfare, examined comparable groups of boys in the Ohio Reform School at Lancaster and of supposedly law-abiding children outside. He found that the inmates of the reformatory had received fully as much religious training as those outside. He concluded that "it seems safe to state that there is no significant relation between religious training and delinquent or non-delinquent behavior. . . ."
>
> Professor Hightower of the University of Iowa, after testing 3,000 children for lying, cheating, and deception, concludes that "there appears to be no relationship of any consequence between Biblical information and the different phases of conduct studies. . . . It indicates very definitely that mere knowledge of the Bible is not in itself sufficient to insure character growth."[4]

I am not saying that religious belief is unrelated to morality. Obviously faith can sustain and anchor our moral ideals as well as move mountains. But this does not mean that adherence to any one religious belief or to any faith at all, as religion is conventionally conceived, is indispensable for moral character. The popular notion puts the cart before the horse.

Character, moral behavior, grows out of a way of life which people not only profess in common but practice in common; and where profession is sincere it is the practice rather than its conscious formulation that is primary in educational growth. Accordingly, if we are genuinely concerned that our children shall acquire habits and ideals of honesty, fair play, self-control, generosity, and respect for the personalities of others, we will have to create conditions of living in home and school and community that embody these ways

[4] Read at Conference on Scientific Spirit and Democratic Faith, New York, May 30, 1943. See *The Arbitrator*, Vol XXV, (July–August), 1943.

of acting, feeling, and thinking. In short, moral ideals as moral practices evolve out of the culture in which men participate. They are rooted in the common and approved ways in which people deal with one another. In so far as religious ideas give body and substance to these assumptions of living, they do so after the fact. As John Stuart Mill long ago pointed out, it is not religion that sustains morality, it is the moral life which men live that prompts them to create, each one for himself, or each group for itself, a religious justification for this behavior. Certainly in a land to which people have come from all parts of the earth in order to better their own lives and the lives of their children, it is a condition of mutual freedom to recognize that morality derives from what men hold and value in common rather than from what distinguishes them as Protestant or Catholic, Jew or Mohammedan, skeptic or atheist.

If this position is sound, the introduction of religious instruction in the schools for the purpose of improving morality may have the result of encouraging the school to neglect or to delegate responsibility for a task that is uniquely its own: that of character development.

Among the profound changes that have taken place in our modern schools in recent years, the most widespread and most valuable has been the attempt to transform schools for schooling into schools for education. The emphasis has shifted from instruction in matters largely verbal to the guidance of boys and girls into experiences of varied types, academic and nonacademic alike, that reorganize and reconstruct experience; that give new quality and substance to their lives; that encourage intelligent ways of seeing, feeling, and acting toward man and nature. The modern school, the progressive school, may have erred at times in practice but its heart has been in the right place. It conceives the primary function of education to be that of providing opportunities for children under guidance to create and re-create their lives.

It is this idea that gives validity to the insistence that the history of American culture should receive more serious attention than of late; provided, of course, that this history be used to refine and temper our standards of living. It likewise sustains the position of those religious liberals who insist that education should develop a framework of values which men can hold in common. But it does not sustain their contention that religious instruction is indispensable for this purpose.

IV

Finally a word needs to be said about the complications with which religious instruction confronts the school administrator.

Suppose he wishes to maintain the scrupulously neutral attitude toward the interests of religious groups that the public character of his school requires. His first problem relates to the enrollment of children in classes in religion. How shall these classes be established and conducted without improper encouraging of one denomination as against another? How can he safeguard the interests of those parents who dissent altogether?

In one community known to me, the school at the beginning of the school year sends a card to the home of each child with instructions for parents to check their preference between two statements: (1) "I wish my child to receive religious instruction"; (2) "I do not wish my child to receive religious instruction." There are, however, only two well-established religious denominations in this community, Roman Catholic and Lutheran. What reply, under the circumstances, should a parent give who does not belong to either one of these church groups? And by what right is the school put in the position of exerting pressure upon minorities on behalf of one or more dominant religious organizations? In this particular community the small number of deviant children in the school are subjected to taunts and jeers on the playground and the street from the children of the major religious groups.

Nor should we overlook the fact that one purpose of the weekday religious school, as its advocates see it, is to bring into the church fold the children of the unchurched. Toward this end, in many a community, the schools are expected to "co-operate." How can the administrator do this without abandoning his neutrality?

Then, too, there is the problem of providing substitute experiences of an educational character for those children who do not attend the religious classes. In some communities the school provides special periods in the arts and crafts, or dramatic play, or special assistance in academic work. But this commonly brings forth objections from religious groups to the effect that it constitutes unfair competition. Similarly the attempt of some schools to provide instruction in ethics during this hour has been interpreted as an unfriendly effort designed to undermine religious instruction.

These objections may seem small-minded. They are; but unfortunately it is the lot of the school administrator, all too often, to encounter molehills endowed with a tendency to develop into mountains.

If it is hard for the school as a whole to avoid entangling alliances in connection with religious instruction, it is equally difficult for teachers, who are in intimate contact with the children, to deal wisely with the issues raised. A recent survey of the operation of the released-time program in New York City, conducted by the Public Education Association, cited many violations of neutrality on the part of teachers—instances in which teachers brought pressure to bear upon children to enroll in religious classes, despite the severe injunctions of administrative authorities to the contrary.

As a result of its study of the actual operation of the released-time program in New York City, the Public Education Association has recommended that the public school be freed from direct responsibility for the enrollment of children in religious classes conducted in religious centers. It suggests that parents and the religious schools should take the initiative in these matters, thus relieving the school of responsibility for the recording and the checking of daily attendance—a task that now consumes hours of public school time and involves considerable expense.

In accordance with these suggestions, parents would request the public school authorities, at stated intervals, to excuse their children from school to attend the church schools. The public school would honor these excuses and dismiss children for the purpose indicated on the days indicated. (In New York this is the last period of the school day on Wednesdays.) At this point the church school would be asked to assume its responsibility as a school, and to become responsible to the parents for the attendance and the conduct of all children enrolled with it.

This arrangement would enlarge the authority and responsibility of the church school, would encourage it to develop closer relations with parents, and would free the public schools from the embarrassing duty of enforcing attendance upon classes over which they have no authority or control.

This plan might reduce the attendance at religious classes, especially in communities where the attendance has depended upon the police power of the public school rather than upon the quality of teaching in the religious school. But by what authority can private agencies use the public schools to maintain their existence? Certainly it is both fair to religious organizations and a matter of plain justice and kindness to the children involved to insist that religious classes survive only so long as they can maintain the loyalty and the co-operation of the parents and the children for whose welfare, presumably, they exist.

v

The introduction of religious instruction into the public schools has been accompanied by attempts, on the part of many Protestant and Catholic groups alike, to secure state support for private and parochial ends. For example, religious forces succeeded, in 1938, in persuading the President's Advisory Committee on Education to recommend that federal funds be used to provide services, such as transportation, for children in non-public schools. Since then state legislatures have been urged—not without success—to pass legislation of this sort: New York State, for instance, has actually authorized the use of state funds for the transportation of children to parochial schools; and efforts have also been made, in New York and other states, to permit state funds to be appropriated for the purchase of textbooks to be used in parochial schools.

Thus are we called upon to define anew the relation of church and state in the sphere of education. An issue that seemed well on its way toward settlement a few years ago elbows its way once more to the fore.

But it is not altogether a case of history repeating itself. Several elements in the problem are new.

For example, the position of the Catholics is different. Some years back it was the objection to the reading of the Protestant Bible in the schools that led Catholics and Jews as well as agnostics to fight for schools free of religious complications. Today Catholics in many localities are endorsing the released-time method of religious instruction, and some of the most vociferous attacks upon our secular schools have come from Catholics. This gives significance to the following words in the Pope's Encyclical addressed to the Church Hierarchy of the United States in October, 1939:

We raise our voice in strong, albeit paternal, complaint that in so many schools of your land Christ is often despised or ignored, the explanation of the Universe and mankind is forced within the narrow limits of materialism or of rationalism, and new educational systems are sought after which cannot but produce a sorrowful harvest in the intellectual and moral life of the nation.

And there is another difference between the contemporary situation and that of a few years ago. As we have seen, it was jealousy and fear on the part of Protestants toward Catholics and Jews that led to early restrictions upon the use of state funds in support of private and parochial schools. They were determined that our government should not aid religious sects which they feared. Today these objections are disappearing as religious groups begin to see advantages in all sharing alike in the bounty of the state. Accordingly many Protestants as well as Catholics are looking to the state for financial assistance for schools of a religious persuasion. Under these conditions it is important to observe that the principle of the separation of church and state in the United States has often meant in practice merely an insistence upon a neutral attitude on the part of the state toward all denominations, not a condition of nonintercourse. In other words, constitutional restrictions and legislation have hitherto grown out of disagreements between sects. Will they survive a period in which private and parochial schools unite in pleas for assistance with which to solve their financial as well as their religious problems?

A few years ago the secular school was enthusiastically acclaimed as an American answer to the problem of educating children of diverse religious, racial, and national backgrounds in a spirit of peace and unity. Today the integrity and validity of this secular school are being challenged. It would be tragic if the challenge succeeded and the result were friction and disunity; and no one, perhaps, would be more dismayed than earnest men and women who are the present proponents of the change.

CHAPTER VII

Our Post-War Responsibility to American Youth

THE war has brought many changes, but none more revolutionary than the transformation in our attitude toward youth. What seemed to be a lost generation has suddenly become the indispensable means of our salvation.

During the depression we faced a serious youth problem. For one thing, young people under twenty-five constituted an abnormally large proportion of our unemployed population; 35 per cent in 1940, as against 22 per cent of the total employable population. Moreover, within the ranks of youth the number of unemployed and out-of-school youth had assumed alarming proportions, as high as 4,000,000 in 1935, out of a total of 21,000,000 youth sixteen to twenty-four years of age.

From whatever point of view we surveyed the future of youth prior to the outbreak of war, we encountered gloomy forebodings. May we glance briefly at the picture.

It was evident that young people were shrinking in numbers proportionately to our middle-aged and old population. Census forecasts indicated a rapid increase for some years to come in the age group of sixty and above, with a tapering off of natural increase and an actual decline by 1950 in the age group of sixteen to twenty-four. These two trends, a diminution in our youth population and an enlargement in the numbers of aged, were already bearing fruit in a competition between old and young for public funds with which to purchase security—a contest in which the older people clearly were beginning to wield the whip hand. Old age pensions and social security were steadily undermining the educational budgets.

Secondly, the younger age groups were being elbowed out of employment. Thus, at the beginning of the century, over 60 per cent of the boys between the ages of fourteen to nineteen were employed as against 35 per cent in 1940. According to census reports in March 1940, 26 per cent of all boys and 23 per cent of all girls in this age group who had joined the labor force were out of work and less than 70 per cent were employed on non-relief jobs. Steadily and consistently employment opportunities for young people under twenty were declining.

To this must be added a third ominous trend. Employment opportunities open to youth were preponderantly blind alley jobs. Between 1935 and the publication of its final report in 1941, the American Youth Commission sampled conditions in every section of the country, rural and urban alike. From these studies two facts stood out: (1) that jobs held by youth were not of the type or the character the young people would freely choose; and (2) the wages and salaries paid were both pitifully low and lacking in assurance for the future.

Such was the status and the prospects of youth in this country when President Roosevelt declared the existence of a national emergency and appealed to the loyalty, the devotion, and the sacrifice of our young people. Well can we understand the dread with which many heard this appeal; their lack of faith in the response of our youth; their fear for the morale of our boys in camp; their doubt of the virility and the courage of a conscript army; their questioning of the ability of our young men "to take" what might be in store for them.

The national emergency is now a state of war. Our country is in danger. Upon the youth of America hinges the salvation not alone of the United States but of the United Nations of the World!

But what of the future? We have every reason to believe that trends of unemployment obtaining prior to the war will re-appear upon the resumption of peace. What do we propose for our youth?

II

There is evidence that the returning veteran will receive generous treatment. Both Congress and the State Legislatures are eager to provide him with adequate facilities for rehabilitation, unemployment insurance, job placement service, preferential status in the civil service, loans with which to purchase a home, a farm or a small business, and, finally, an opportunity to continue his education or training at the point where he left off when he joined the military forces.

The Servicemen's Readjustment Act of 1944 provides in substance as follows for the education of men or women who have been honorably discharged from military and naval service:

(1) Any honorably discharged veteran who was twenty-five years of age or less at the time of entering military or naval service may receive one year's training at virtually any type of general or specialized educational institution the individual selects, including elementary or secondary school, college, business, scientific or technical institution, vocational and professional school, apprenticeship and job training establishment.

(2) "Upon satisfactory completion of such course of education or training, according to the regularly prescribed standards and practices of the institutions, except a refresher or retraining course, such person shall be entitled to an additional period or periods of education or training, not to exceed the time such person was in active service on or after September 16, 1940, and before the termination of the war, exclusive of any period he was assigned for a course of education or training under the Army specialized training program or the Navy college training program, which course was a continuation of his civilian course and was pursued to completion, or as a cadet or midshipman at one of the service

academies." In no event, however, may the total period of education or training exceed four years.

(3) For this purpose the government will provide individuals allowances of $50 per month for board, lodging, and other living expenses if single; and $75 per month if married, with $10 additional for each dependent child. Moreover, tuition (up to $500) and fees will be met by the government.

(4) Educational and vocational guidance will be available to veterans with respect to their continued education. Moreover, the Veterans' Administration will make available to veterans, from time to time, "information respecting the need for general education and for trained personnel in the various crafts, trades, and professions."

(5) An administrative agency within the Veterans Administration is charged with responsibility for carrying out these plans in cooperation with the armed forces and the several states.

Generous as these provisions are, they do not distinguish sufficiently between the needs of the various age groups that have gone into the army. One year's education with government assistance for a boy who entered the army fresh from high school will not take him far in preparation for civilian life whereas a year for a man about to conclude his professional training is all that he requires. It would seem necessary to supplement assistance for the younger men, at least for those of limited resources, with some provision analogous to the student aid provided needy young by the N.Y.A. in the years preceding the war.

III

But what of the demobilized worker? What do we contemplate for the boys and girls who entered industry at fourteen to seventeen? How can we safeguard them from being cast upon the industrial scrap-heap? Surely this is a national problem of first magnitude. What is being done to cope with it?

Thus far, nothing. Indeed, worse than nothing, since the federal machinery painfully developed prior to the war to serve unemployed youth was abandoned under the cloak of the war emergency.

For example, an organization called the Citizens' Emergency Committee on Non-Defense Expenditures was quick to seize upon the fact of war to urge the elimination of government services to youth and the unfortunate. With a prominent educator as chairman, it recommended early in 1942 the discontinuance of the Civilian Conservation Corps and the National Youth Administration. It was likewise ready to predict (we will not say hopefully but certainly with little appreciation of the needs of young people in wartime) that "schools, parks, and playgrounds, child welfare, health protection—may be found to be luxuries which the ordinary community can no longer afford."

Similarly, less than three weeks following the attack on Pearl Harbor, the Joint Committee of Congress on Reduction of Non-Essential Federal Expenditures, rendered a preliminary report on its assigned task of investigating "all expenditures of the Federal Government, with a view to recommending the elimination or reduction of all such expenditures deemed by the Committee to be non-essential." This Committee looked first to relief and to agencies serving youth for substantial savings. On the ground that "There is no room for non-essentials in a government stripped for action," the Committee suggested the liquidation of the Civilian Conservation Corps and the National Youth Administration as early as possible.

The recommendations of the Joint Committee received substantial support from the Congress elected in November 1943. The Civilian Conservation Corps was quickly liquidated. Then followed the National Youth Administration despite the fact that upon the declaration of war this agency concentrated upon the training of young people for work

in defense industries. Indeed in the last months of its existence the National Youth Administration was preparing some
30,000 young people each month for defense work as its
contribution toward a critical shortage of workers.

We thus face the post-war period without any present
assurance that young people's needs will be met by the Federal Government. Competent judges who know at first-hand
the work of the National Youth Administration in its counselling and guidance services, its residential centers and its
production work shops, considered this organization a model
for meeting the special problems of a group for whom
schools had previously made no provision—young people
out-of-school and past the age of compulsory school attendance. Had our government continued the National Youth
Administration in skeleton form with an eye to its post-war
functions we might confront the problems of demobilized
youth with an easier mind than is now possible.

Let us glance briefly at the picture.

It is difficult to state exactly how many young persons are
at work today since the last census was taken in the early
spring of 1940 and the numbers employed have changed
rapidly. However, rough estimates of the U. S. Department
of Labor would indicate that there are between 2,000,000 and
3,000,000 young people of 18 years and less now employed
in contrast with something over 900,000 in 1940.

There is an ominous note in these winds of change. Enrollments in secondary schools are falling rapidly. Child labor
is on the increase and the protection once afforded children
by the slow evolution of child labor laws is no longer effective.

For example, the Children's Bureau reports that not only
are more young people entering labor's ranks but this increase
is greater within the age-range of 14 and 15 than it is within
that of 16 to 17. In October of 1943 there were 2,750,000
children at work. Of these 750,000 were 14 and 15—one of

every six of this age in the total population—and 2,000,000 were 16 and 17—two out of every five of these ages.[1]

Nor do these figures include the large number of children illegally employed. How many comprise this group no one knows. According to Katherine Lenroot, chief of the Children's Bureau, however, "violations both of State child labor laws and of the child labor provisions of the Federal Fair Labor Standards Act have increased alarmingly."

It is evident that we are building up a huge army of young people who may constitute a rudderless group following the war. The highly fractionated operations in which they engage in war industries will have little carry-over value for peace-time occupations. They are untrained and uneducated, but having tasted adult life they will not consent to step back into the ranks of school children. How do we propose to deal with this newest, and, in some respects, most acute problem in American life today?

The first essential is to recognize that in one sense it is not new. It is rather the culmination of long-time trends that we have every reason to believe will reassert themselves with the resumption of peace. We refer to the steady exclusion of children from gainful occupations and the consequent substitution of schooling. Were we to construct two tables covering the past forty or fifty years, one to illustrate, as it would, the steady exclusion of young people below twenty from work and the other as it also would do, the phenomenal increase of enrollments first in elementary schools, then in secondary schools and finally in technical schools and colleges, we would observe that these two supplement each other. Not immediately, or line by line, since school attendance lags a bit behind the obvious need for it. But the interval is not long since, on the whole, Americans have met the problem of unemployment first of children and second of youth

[1] See in this connection *Wartime Employment of Boys and Girls under 18*. Publication 289, U. S. Dept. of Labor, Children's Bureau, 1943.

by insisting, through compulsory school attendance laws, that the schools provide education as work opportunities disappeared.[2]

This necessity of adapting the school program to ever new groups of young people explains why educators seemed perpetually engaged in reorganizing their schools. No sooner were adjustments made in the school program for one age level than an influx of new elements into the school population demanded further adaptations in the curriculum. For example, the junior high school movement in the second decade of this century reflected the fact that mass education was no longer the sole responsibility of the elementary school. The high school was now asked to provide something in the way of education for all. Consequently educators began to provide "terminal" education in the junior high school, and a combined general and vocational training roughly analogous to that now advocated for public junior colleges resulted. Few educators justify today vocational training in the junior high. Why? Because business and industry, prior to the war, quite generally excluded young people between the ages of sixteen and twenty just as in the second decade of this century they excluded children of elementary school age. Consequently we seek new instruments with which to meet the needs of an age group for whom there is every reason to believe, when peace comes, there will be few opportunities for work and only meager educational provision.

Many who see in this delayed participation of youth in

[2] Paul T. David states, "With increasing industrialization, the proportion of gainfully occupied boys from 16 to 19 increased until 1910; then a decline set in which became rapid after 1920. The proportion of gainfully occupied girls from 16 to 19, however, increased until 1920, following which it declined. . . . Between 1920 and 1940, the age group 16 and 17 years old was rapidly being assimilated into the pattern of general school attendance, and members of the age group from 18 to 20 were remaining in school and attending college in increasing numbers." For more complete detail, see chapter on Industrial and Occupational Trends in *Postwar Youth Employment*, Prepared for The American Youth Commission, The American Council on Education, Washington, D. C., 1943.

the world's work an ultimate blessing, precisely as it has enriched childhood and early adolescence, are proposing an extension of general education to the age group of sixteen to twenty, just as, some years ago, they advocated similar provisions for children under sixteen.

This does not mean an immediate raising of the age of compulsory school attendance, although the leaving age in a number of states is doubtless too low. Enforced attendance upon school is neither the wisest method to enduce youth to value education nor a safe guarantee that the schools will adapt their programs to the peculiar needs of the young people thus required to attend. It does mean, however, that Americans should concentrate immediately upon plans for the free education, under public auspices, of essentially a new group in public education.

Some of these young people will, of course, follow the customary channels of education in college, higher technical schools and professional institutions. A continued expansion of these facilities, along lines interrupted by the war, with perhaps a more vigorous development of junior colleges, will serve the purpose of an increasing proportion of high school graduates.

Young people who left school prior to graduation in order to engage in temporary war jobs constitute a more acute problem. Unless safeguarded they may constitute a frustrated and lost generation.

In a recent publication for the American Youth Commission,[3] Paul T. David points out that long-term industrial and occupational trends indicate a declining need for unskilled labor "and that the occupational prospects of the unskilled laborers as a group can be improved only to the extent that they can be upgraded into other occupations." Consequently neither society nor the individuals concerned can leave to chance the matter of these young people finding a place in

[3] *Postwar Youth Employment*, Ch. III. American Council on Education, Washington, D. C., 1943.

our industrial order when peace comes and jobs disappear into thin air.

The first step in meeting the needs peculiar to this group is doubtless to establish a counselling and guidance service analogous to that once furnished by the N.Y.A. This service might well perform the dual function of job placement, where possible, and guidance, so that assistance in meeting economic needs is followed with guidance of a more personal character in which individuals are directed toward appropriate vocational skills, hobbies and the constructive use of leisure. As the Committee on Post-War Adult Education in New York City has wisely suggested, the educational needs evidenced by people using a counselling service of this character would throw light on the type of educational programs best adapted for them.

One point is clear. Neither the conventional day school nor the typical evening school program as they now operate seem organized to attract our young people. For example, despite the fact that there are more than 3,000,000 adults in New York City who have gone no farther than the eighth grade, the average daily attendance upon evening elementary, secondary and trade schools is only 23,490. We must insure, of course, vocational training and retraining courses for young people as well as an open door for the ambitious and the able to obtain a general education leading on to college and technical school. But to this we must add a type of general education not yet fully developed, analogous perhaps to the Danish Folk School that acquainted young men and women with the history, the literature, the music and the art of their culture in a manner appropriate to the psychology and the maturity of young adults. A number of the N.Y.A. residential centers had developed suggestive programs of this character prior to their abandonment. A few workers' schools have also contributed toward this end. Data from these experiments will have to be searched out and promising possibilities tried out on a larger scale. Of prime importance is to realize that indispensable and central as vocational preparation truly is, the emotional and social needs of later adolescence overflow the vocational motive. We cannot leave to accident and chance preparation for the fruitful use of leisure, the intelligent functions of citizenship, relations with the opposite sex that promise a satisfying marriage, or the knowledge of child care essential for healthy family life.

How shall we provide these new educational services? Can we wait upon local initiative or shall we turn to the Federal Government to supplement and perhaps give direction to local effort? This question brings us face to face with the problem of federal intervention in education.

At present both economy groups inside and outside of Congress together with large numbers of educators, represented by the Educational Policies Commission of the National Education Association, are opposed to federal direction in education. Indeed a report issued by the Educational Policies Commission in November, 1941[4] marshalled the powerful resources of the National Education Association behind efforts to abolish the federal agencies then serving American youth. The Commission believed the existence of the C.C.C. and the N.Y.A. foreshadowed the building of a dual system of education in this country: one supported and controlled by states and localities; the other by the Federal Government. Not only did the Commission see this encouraging competition for funds (in the event the Federal Government grants sums with which to equalize educational opportunities in the various states) but it feared it would likewise encourage opening the door for officials in Washington to control the minds of young people dependent upon them for educational advantages. Accordingly the Commission urged rigid adherence to the time-honored principle of local autonomy in American education.

[4] *The Civilian Conservation Corps, the National Youth Administration and the Public Schools.*

In brief the recommendations of the Commission were as follows:

(1) That the Federal Government appropriate funds for student aid, these funds to be distributed by the Office of Education to schools, colleges, and universities through appropriate state agencies.

(2) That the functions of the N.Y.A. be continued but be carried on under state and local auspices with the help of federal appropriations.

(3) That the opportunities for education in the several states be equalized through the appropriation of federal funds to the Office of Education. The Office of Education should distribute these funds to the States on the basis of objective criteria to "be determined by such definite and ascertainable factors as the number of children and youth to be educated and the fiscal capacity of the state to educate them."

(4) As against federal control and direction of youth programs, the Commission would rely upon leadership emanating from the Office of Education to develop and stimulate a program of education for youth within the age-range of seventeen to twenty-four "through research, conference, experimentation, demonstration, publication."

What shall we say to these suggestions?

First we must observe, regretfully, that the Commission's report, backed as it was by the endorsement of well-known educators, served as excellent grist for the mills of those who hoped to extinguish altogether the federal youth agencies. The Commission recommended the replacement of agencies already functioning under federal auspices by state or local programs not then in operation; and it hoped to support these non-existent programs with federal funds to be appropriated under the stringent conditions of a wartime economy. The allies of the educators in Congress voted merely to abolish the federal agencies.

With what result? Neither the Federal government nor

the states and localities now possess the machinery with which to minister to the post-war needs of several million young people between the ages of twelve and seventeen who have withdrawn from school and entered what may be for them the blind alley occupations of war industries!

Let us turn to the suggestions of the Commission as they bear upon the post-war problems of young people.

The first two recommendations seem to have in mind two quite different classes of American youth: in the first instance needy students normally enrolled in school and college who require only financial assistance in order to pursue the "regular" curriculum, and in the second young people analogous to those for whom the N.Y.A. attempted to provide both work experience and vocational education and training.

As to the first, no one who believes the Federal government should help to equalize educational opportunity will object to the appropriation of funds designed to enable worthy boys and girls to continue their education in school and college. Moreover the suggestion that the Office of Education control and administer the distribution of these funds seems consistent with the functions of a national office of education.

The assistance rendered needy students in the past by the N.Y.A. and the inauguration of an educational plan for veterans presage future extensions of the principle of federal aid in the education and training of worthy young people. Bread thus cast upon the waters will surely return before many days.

The first recommendation of the Educational Policies Commission is thus suggestive of a plan that is applicable both to the period of demobilization and to normal conditions of peace.

The second recommendation; namely, that the functions heretofore performed by the C.C.C. and the N.Y.A. be carried on under state and local auspices, is less praiseworthy.

Note first that this recommendation presupposes much

more than federal aid on behalf of the equalization of educational opportunities. No one, we hope, who is acquainted with the educational needs of young people in our country where wealth and opportunity vary so markedly from state to state, will oppose efforts to secure federal funds designed to equalize educational facilities. Obviously the neglect of education in one state works to the disadvantage of living conditions in another. Thus poverty and lack of opportunity in the southern states, with a high birth rate, result in a steady migration of young people each year to the north, with deleterious effects upon both standards of living and upon what Dr. John L. Elliott once termed standards of living together. Malnutrition at any point in our body politic, like malnutrition in the physical body, results inevitably in lowering resistance to disease and fatigue and in hampering efficiency.

Let us suppose, however, that Congress were convinced of the necessity of equalizing educational opportunities in the elementary and secondary schools of the states through federal aid. The type of young people once served by the C.C.C. and the N.Y.A. would still remain unprovided for, since these agencies dealt only with out-of-school youth between the ages of seventeen and twenty-four. In short, the Educational Policies Commission suggested the abandonment of federal agencies then serving a distinctive age group in communities throughout the United States on the assumption that states and localities would develop substitute facilities despite the fact that it was their failure, in the first instance to bestir themselves that led to federal action!

Certainly attempts to equalize educational opportunities within the states through Federal grants to elementary and secondary schools carries no assurance that the states will provide better than heretofore for the needs of youth above the age of compulsory school attendance. But it is precisely this age group that is affected by the proposal to assign the functions once performed by the N.Y.A. to local agencies. The Commission apparently overlooked also the practical situation that will obtain in the post-war period. Federal grants must follow upon rather than antedate well-established evidence of local need. They will at best keep step with a slow, gradual evolution and development of educational programs within the various states and localities, many of which are now retarded in the extreme. If our policy is to wait upon local initiative, what assurance have we that a problem national in its scope will be solved? On what basis can we assume that federal funds in sufficient amounts will be made speedily available to public schools? Or, if appropriated, that a sufficient number of schools will possess either the vision, the originality, the personnel, or the facilities with which to meet the crisis?

Moreover, employment needs and retraining needs of young people between eighteen and twenty-five vary markedly with conditions. To meet them flexibility is required and an organization that can expand or contract widely. This suggests an administrative unit larger than the customary school system. Indeed a federal organization analogous to the N.Y.A. constitutes an admirable agency for this purpose. It is regrettable that Congress did not see fit to continue this agency with a skeleton personnel ready to meet post-war conditions. Surely past experience indicates clearly that only by means of an organization and administration embracing an area larger than one state can we hope to cope with the critical conditions certain to confront us. In this connection the observations of Floyd Reeves are peculiarly pertinent. He states,

The national youth programs should be federally administered, because most local and many state taxing units do not have the fiscal ability to support such an enterprise, and also because a federal institution can more quickly adjust itself to the prompt and large-scale expansion and contraction necessitated by private employment fluctuations.

Fear of federal administration of education operates also to weaken the Commission's recommendations with respect to the control and direction of grants of federal funds to states and localities. It suggests that educational opportunities in the states be equalized through the appropriation of federal funds to the Office of Education. The Office of Education would distribute these funds to the states on the basis of objective criteria to "be determined by such definite and ascertainable factors as the number of children and youths to be educated and the fiscal capacity of the state to educate them." The Commission vaguely envisages some central control over the use of these funds by state and local agencies but would limit the character of the control. Thus it states, "It is to be expected that federal grants-in-aid for a comprehensive program of education would specify the general purposes for which federal funds were to be expended. Such earmarkings would be desirable for a limited period, sufficiently long to permit the newer types of services to become firmly established in the public educational systems."

The dilemma that confronts the Commission is the one that troubles all who seek to solve problems common to large areas solely through local instrumentalities. Obviously, if the Office of Education were permitted to control too firmly the distribution of federal funds, a federal plan of education might develop. Consequently the Commission treads lightly and recommends merely that the Office of Education exercise "leadership" through research, demonstration, and publication. The Office of Education is to remain an office and an office only!

It is doubtful that this scheme would insure either the wisest use of federal funds or the soundest leadership. Does it not assume that leadership is best exercised without specific responsibility?

This brings us face to face with the hobgoblin of federal control of education. Since the days of our founding fathers the dogma of local autonomy has flourished in education no less vigorously than the dictum of states rights in the political field. Aiding and abetting this principle has been the fear of a central government and the power it might exercise over men's minds. But just as the principle of state sovereignty operates in politics to retard legislation designed to alleviate general social and economic conditions, so in education it now stands in the way of an impartial and objective study of the most effective means for serving the youth of the entire nation.

It should be clear, for example, that there are areas in which generally accepted principles will have to receive educational support over wide areas, even to the extent of running counter to local prejudices and local conviction. Surely at a time when the United Nations are considering seriously some form of international control over post-war education in Germany, in order to avoid a resurgence of Nazi doctrines of intolerance and aggression, the people of the United States should give thought to their own principles of local autonomy and unrestricted freedom of instruction.

In a challenging article entitled "Plans for Peace Must Include Education," James Marshall, a member of the New York City Board of Education, has drawn attention to the method employed by the Scandinavian nations to lay the basis for peace between their peoples, following centuries of warfare. A commission was authorized to edit text books in each country with a view to removing material detrimental to good-will. With this as an object lesson, Marshall suggests:

If the teaching materials in the schools and children's books are to bring peoples to a better understanding of each other, are to teach nations to be companionable, they require sympathetic editing by an instrumentality similar to that which worked so successfully among the Scandinavian countries. Here is an important task for an international education office.

With plans of this character in mind to promote peace and good will between nations can we neglect similar efforts to breed tolerance and understanding, a conviction of a shared culture and common opportunities as between racial and religious groups within a nation? Within, that is to say, these

United States, where subtle and insidious forces are bent upon stirring up hate and suspicion between groups? Shall we carry the principle of *laissez faire* in education to the point that schools in backward areas (in our great cities as well as in remote and undernourished rural areas) are permitted to develop in children ideas of false inferiority and superiority and to stir up fears and antagonisms based upon religious, economic, racial, and cultural differences?

We shall not attempt to answer these questions at this time. Our purpose is rather to stress the point that *laissez faire* is as difficult a policy to follow today in the dissemination of ideas as it is in the distribution of goods and services. And, further, it is becoming clear that in the very process of safeguarding local freedom we may have to institute general controls that overarch the individual states.

Our traditional fear of a central government and, as a consequence, the determination to prohibit the Federal Government from participation in education, derives from a conception of the state no longer appropriate to a modern democracy. Government was once an external, often an arbitrary, agency unconcerned with the vital concerns of the governed. With improved communications on the one hand and a conception of interdependence that enables people to function fruitfully in the lives of others, a more intimate relationship between a government and its people has evolved. Our government is an extension of our own interests and concerns. It is the organized expression, the vehicle, of a people's will, designed to realize cooperatively ends that cannot be realized in isolation. Fear of government as such derives from an age in which government signified rule, not service. It dates from a period of arbitrary restraint and regulation antedating the creation through democratic means of common devices for ministering sensitively to men's needs.

Unfortunately some governments in the twentieth century have revived ancient tyrannies. But the remedy is not to pulverize the relations that bind men together. It is rather to search out ways and means in which associated action can serve needs without enslaving people in the process. In the field of education, this suggests a careful determination of those areas in which federal participation, beyond the mere payment of bills, can safely be encouraged and those areas in which initiative and variation should be lodged exclusively within localities and states.

As a matter of fact, neither a centralized system of education, administered solely from Washington, nor an irresponsible type of state and local education (even with opportunities financially equalized) is adapted to contemporary conditions of American life. State lines no longer constitute the normal and natural boundary lines for the effective administration of education on behalf of young people between the ages of seventeen and twenty-five. The National Youth Administration recognized this fact in its administrative organization. Consequently it lodged genuine responsibility for local adaptation and variation in its regional directors with the help of advisory boards, and it organized regional supervisory districts that often cut across state lines. It thus recognized the need for close coordination between locality, region and nation.

Here we have the germs of an administrative organization for education that seems to avoid both the evils of an exclusively state and local administration and a federal control insensitive to local peculiarities and needs. At the same time, should it not stimulate a marshalling of opportunities for youth that today lie fallow in the barren soil of a backward and unenlightened state or locality? Were the Federal Government to encourage the organization of educational services for youth on a regional basis under broad general directives addressed to regional boards (composed in part of state educational officials from the states involved and in part of laymen possessed of public vision), a unique combination of federal and regional administration might emerge.

Interstate or regional organizations of this character would insure freedom from federal "domination" at the same time that they promoted educational planning and cooperation between localities and states that are now only too prone to dwell in self-contented backwardness. Indeed, the mere existence of such an over-all administrative organization in regions where common needs overflow state lines might stimulate creative planning after the pattern of joint projects already engaged in by a number of states (notably the Port Authority of New York and New Jersey) outside the field of education.

But whether we meet the needs of young people above the age of seventeen through federal instrumentalities or the much slower method of state action, we should recognize the critical nature of the problem they pose for our future. Nowhere does there exist at present adequate provision for young people at this very critical age who are neither in school nor normally employed. This is the age when youth demands adult status. Young people wish to stand on their own feet and to direct their own lives. They are eager to establish homes of their own and they know that in order to do so they must have work and some assurance of future advancement. In the Army they have become accustomed to good food, clothing, shelter, and fairly generous provision for study or play and recreation in their leisure hours. In industry they have tasted the fruits of steady work and what tolerable wages can buy. They have observed that crises in our economic and our social life can be met through government intervention and they suspect that unemployment and poverty need not exist. Both those who are in the national service and those now in national industry have responded to their country's call at a time of grave national danger. Let peace come without intelligent plan or provision for an open road along which they can travel hopefully, and there will be no peace. Should these young people conclude from our neglect that our faith in democracy and freedom is a faith without works, non-applicable to them, who will say that they will not rise up in their wrath, as did Samson of old, to destroy the pillars of the society that so cruelly played them false?

CHAPTER VIII

Should Our Schools Indoctrinate?

PRIOR to 1930 complacency characterized much of the work in school and college alike. The issues of education upon which educators centered were largely those of detail. Viewed in retrospect, they seem trivial indeed; quite in contrast with those brought to the fore by the 1930's.

To George Counts, in large measure, belongs the credit for sounding an awakening bell in the ears of self-satisfied educators and laymen, with the publication in April, 1932 of a pamphlet on "Dare the Schools Build a New Social Order?"[1]

Counts answered his query by stating that while schools will scarcely succeed in building a new social order, nevertheless the attempt to do so constitutes the main business of education in a democracy. He attacked boldly the insipid liberalism of the open mind, void of fundamental convictions, and issued a clarion call to the teachers of the nation to assume the professional responsibility of moulding the minds of the on-coming generation.

Assuming [he said] that the child will be imposed upon in some fashion by the various elements in his environment, the real question is not whether imposition will take place, but rather from what source will it come.

Accordingly, he urged teachers to organize as a guild, pointing out that,

Through powerful organizations they might at least reach the public conscience and come to exercise a larger measure of con-

[1] This consisted of several addresses delivered earlier in the year to national groups of educators.

trol over the schools than hitherto. They would then have to assume some responsibility for the more fundamental forms of imposition which, according to my argument, cannot be avoided.

This challenge permeated educational circles throughout the nation. Nor was interest confined to the professional educator. The economic foundations of our society seemed to be crumbling under the weakening effects of a world-wide depression. Many feared that old faiths as well as old institutions would give way to what Anne Lindbergh later characterized the "wave of the future."

But who should give character to the wave of the future? Or, better, by what method should we select from possible future trends the one entitled to orthodox standing in the American school? Liberals were not wanting to oppose Counts' conclusion. They urged on the behalf of democracy, that there be no indoctrination in the schools. The ideal of a free education is realized, they insisted, only when teacher and students employ an inquiring mind, using hypotheses in the study of social and economic questions with the same unbiased attitude that the scientist exercises in his investigations of the phenomena of nature. On the other hand, groups, influenced by the progress of the Russian revolution and still others by fascism in Italy and Germany, readily accepted Counts' major assumption that indoctrination is the primary function of education and proceeded "to bore within" the extracurricular as well as the curricular structure of American schools and colleges.

Much of this discussion on indoctrination reminds one, in retrospect, of an incident which William James describes in one of his essays. James refers to a metaphysical argument that occupied the idle hours of a camping party in the Adirondack Mountains.

The corpus of the dispute was a squirrel—a live squirrel supposed to be clinging to one side of a tree-trunk; while over against the tree's opposite side a human being was imagined to stand. This human witness tries to get sight of the squirrel by moving rapidly round the tree, but no matter how fast he goes, the squirrel moves as fast in the opposite direction, and always keeps the tree between himself and the man, so that never a glimpse of him is caught. The resultant metaphysical problem now is this: Does the man go round the squirrel or not?

James attempted to settle the problem by indicating that the controversy was conditional solely upon employing the term "goes round" in two senses and shuttling from one to the other without notice.

So it is with the issue of indoctrination in education. With this difference; for James and his friends the debate served merely to while away idle vacation hours. Teachers and parents, on the other hand, who endeavor to come seriously to terms with the issue of indoctrination will go far toward clarifying the responsibility of an older to a younger generation. We can settle this issue satisfactorily only when we have made explicit in our minds the theory of learning we wish to use in dealing with young people, and the relations of the individual to society we desire to obtain. For example, those who follow the behaviorists in believing that human beings are as putty to be "conditioned" according to preconceived or existing patterns, will settle the question of indoctrination without difficulty. For them, indoctrination is a fact, not a hypothetical program. They hold with Nathaniel Peffer,

When indoctrination for a new social order is practicable it will no longer be necessary, for then the new order will have surrendered or been converted. Whatever education may be culturally or as a concept, as an institution it is not independent or self-sufficient. It cannot create; it can only reflect. It cannot generate new social ideas; it can transmit only those which are already accepted. It must always bend to the collective will around it.[2]

On the other hand, those who conceive of growing up in more organic terms, insist that the indoctrinators oversimplify; that they apply to the whole range of human learn-

[2] *Harper's Magazine*, January, 1934.

ing and experience facts that hold true of at best a small segment. This group believes that young and old are genuinely creative in large areas of conduct and behavior; that these creative experiences embody both the quality of the individual and the substance of his surroundings, much as an artist evolves something genuinely new and original out of the blending of his materials with the ideas he seeks to express. Accordingly, for these educators, the problem of education in home and school becomes that of helping children to acquire a stock of varied resources in the way of ideas and habits, dispositions and attitudes, some of which may reflect rather faithfully elements in the cultural milieu, and others will constitute distinctive, unique, and flexible deviations from accepted codes of behavior and conventional patterns of thought.

Before we commit ourselves to either one of these conflicting conceptions of learning, let us imitate James's caution and inspect the common meanings of the word *indoctrination*. It derives from the Latin, *doctrino*, to teach. The dictionary definition "To instruct in doctrines or principles in general, or in those of some one branch of learning or system of belief; instruct; teach" seems benevolently neutral. But if we refer to practice and observe what usually takes place where instruction is given in systems of religious belief, we know that more is aimed at and expected than a mere knowledge about the tenets of a faith. Acceptance of the dogmas on the part of the learner is alone satisfactory.

With this as a clue, a clean-cut definition of indoctrination seems to emerge. It consists in the instilling of a specific belief or developing a specific habit, attitude, or disposition under conditions in which attention centers primarily upon beliefs, attitudes, and dispositions as end results. That is to say, we do not indoctrinate *in general*. We indoctrinate only when we seek to mould, or to convince, or to convert the learner in a perfectly definite and preconceived manner; and, secondly, we indoctrinate when we recognize that the thing learned or acquired is of greater importance than the *method* employed to attain the goal.

By thus pinning down the meaning of the word, we are in a position to define our position with reference to the method of indoctrination. Few of us will question, for example, the necessity of employing it in some areas of life with children "before the age of discretion." We can hardly reason with the babe regarding the relative merits of nursing or artificial feeding. The situation and his elders will have to decide this momentous issue. Similarly, habits of personal hygiene and in the course of time, facts such as those of addition and subtraction, the dates and events of history, the location of places in geography and huge blocks of equally arbitrary experience arrange themselves under this category. To become indoctrinated, to accept passively, to reflect faithfully aspects of life about us, is one of the prices we pay for the privilege of living with others. Consequently, if we were to draw a scale of learning in the form of a straight line running from the left side of a paper to the right, we should indicate upon it a considerable section as belonging legitimately to indoctrination.

Pure indoctrination.	Indoctrination with content somewhat variable.	The disputed area. Facts and truths uncertain with emotions deeply involved. Indoctrination desired by some.	Facts relative. Progress dependent upon pure method. NO indoctrination desired.

One space to the right of pure indoctrination would provide for traits of character and principles of conduct such as honesty, trustworthiness, and other virtues which constitute the social cement of all human groupings. These characteristics are peculiar to no one state of society or level of culture. To be sure, the specific content of an act, such as honesty, will vary with time and place, and will confront us with the necessity from time to time of reinterpreting and enlarging its meaning; but even so a relatively stable body of conduct survives the vicissitudes of time and place and no practical parent or teacher can avoid indoctrinating children to some extent in these virtues. Although we may wish for increasingly intelligent methods of teaching we recognize that the outcome, the goal, is always of greater significance than the means used in reaching it.

Now let us jump to the extreme right on our scale. This calls for precisely the opposite of indoctrination. The teacher of science, for example, who best fulfils his function equips his students with refined *methods* for arriving at conclusions rather than with an unquestioned allegiance to theories, concepts, and facts. Here the process of reaching conclusions, the logic peculiar to the field of inquiry in science, mathematics, history, and the like, an abiding loyalty to the search for truth as against whole-hearted devotion to a particular conclusion or theory are essential for success. The emotions, so fundamentally important in the previous instances, are at this point a source of danger and error. Truth for its own sake is our exclusive goal. The scientist or the scholar at all worth his salt has learned with John Locke that

To be indifferent which of two opinions is true, is the right temper of mind that preserves it from being imposed on, and disposes it to examine with that indifferency till it has done its best to find the truth; and this is the only direct and safe way to it.

One space on our line to the left of that signifying pure inquiry represents the No-Man's Land of controversial issues. This space would include beliefs and theories and dogmas by their very nature uncertain, but, nevertheless upon whose truth or falsity depend often the issues of life. But here, too, our emotions are most intimately intertwined with the outcome. So it is that we are tempted by dogmatism and intolerance, and are deluded into believing that acceptance in some manner insures validity. Consequently the experimental method, dear to the scientist's heart as scientist, is refused application to a moral or a social theory. The caliber of his thinking changes when he deals with an economic or political theory as yet untried and certainly not verified; when he is forced to redefine his attitude toward a practice hallowed by time but questioned by changes in circumstances that once justified and gave purpose to it. Indeed, it would seem as though in this uncertain area emotional disturbance and the abandonment of rational procedure varied inversely with men's subconscious confidence in the validity of their views! And, at the same time, it is precisely at these points of valid doubt that mistakes in judgment and action following emotion and bias are most tragic in their consequences. Upon the heads of the innocent are visited the sins of bigots and indoctrinators!

The objections to indoctrination are fairly obvious.

In the first place, there is the danger of perpetuating social lag. Nor does this apply exclusively to conservatives. An examination of the programs put forth by reformers in the LaFollette, Roosevelt, and Wilson era reveals the fact that frequently they grounded their measures upon an analysis of an earlier period, with the result that their efforts at reform were cut to the pattern of an economic and industrial order already in process of transformation. This tendency to revert to the past is perhaps inevitable, and in those realms of activity where change is not overly significant, an appeal to the funded experience of the race is of great value. But to impose upon young people our specific solutions for the maladjustments of a changing society may result only in loading them down with useless luggage.

A second reason for avoiding indoctrination in disputed areas of knowledge is the fact that our pet solutions for the ills of the present may be no more than retreats from reality. The distinctive features of a Utopia are usually the points of greatest misfit in the present, and the major items in our dreams of the New Jerusalem are commonly our compromises with and our ways of escaping from the evils of the moment. Theories of this character glide conveniently over the realities and complexities of actual situations. The peculiarities of culture and tradition that distinguish a country such as the United States from other countries are likely to be ignored in favor of a way of life which, when viewed from afar, seems to guarantee to us the values we hold dear.

But indoctrination is questionable mainly because of the violence it may do to the integrity of child nature. Being young signifies a form of disinterestedness, a peculiar detachment from the interests and concerns that warp the minds and cramp the emotional nature of adults. Against this society can ill afford to sin. It represents an opportunity to start anew, to plow virgin soil and to plant seeds that promise variations from old practices. Rather than to mould the thoughts of young people solely in the image of our prejudices, we should strive to assist them to acquire a large measure of flexibility.

One way of attaining this end is to help young people to distinguish between loyalty to a principle of conduct and its specific applications. Thus we may consider the acceptance of social responsibility for assuring to all members of society the minimum essentials of food, clothing, and shelter as indispensable in a civilized existence. We might even agree that this should constitute a basic principle meriting indoctrination, and yet the means for its realization in practice will vary with place and circumstances. It is not identical, for example, with provision for old age pensions or unemployment insurance, since these are necessarily relevant to a particular time and a particular state of economic development.

This distinction between a general principle and its concrete embodiment, when clearly maintained, enables the teacher to steer a safe course between improper propagandizing on behalf of his own views and an empty and insipid liberalism that often passes for the open mind.

But how can we assure ourselves that children are holding

fast to stable principles of thought and action in variable applications?

In the first place, by helping them to organize their work and play life in harmony with them. If noncompetitive motives, for example, cannot find expression in children's games, in classroom projects, in shared experiences with brother and sister, and schoolmate and friend, instruction on behalf of a substitute for the profit motive in industry will fall upon deaf ears and will have little influence upon the pupil's subsequent conduct in business. On the other hand, it is possible to incorporate in the life of the school and the home the principles we wish to animate increasingly the world of affairs. Frequently the parallel is obvious, and young people can themselves sense the implications of their decisions. Thus the editorial board of a high school paper confronts in a small way the problems of newspaper management in its advertising policy. Shall it assume responsibility for the influence of its advertisements upon the readers of the paper or shall it subscribe to the doctrine of read-at-your-own-risk? Similarly, in athletic and recreational programs. Playing to win as against the love of the game; granting special privileges for the purpose of building up athletic prowess in the student body; awarding prizes which cause pupils to compete as individuals against individuals; promoting forms of student government and extra-curricular activities to devise and practice the methods of a Tammany politician, tend to perpetuate attitudes toward life characteristic of an individualistic era. Step by step and point by point the school will have to provide ways of living that give zest and meaning and significance to everyday work and play experiences, but which accord with more generous living values.

Training for international-mindedness and education for peace may further illustrate our point. As against the temptation to indoctrinate children directly with the advantages of peace we can feed generously their curiosity regarding other people. This curiosity in the ways of people in the far away and the long ago serves as a means for enabling children to approach sympathetically and understandingly the customs and habits and life values of those who differ from them. The study of history and of contemporary civilization is thus an admirable tool for wearing down provincialism and an exaggerated and belligerent satisfaction in our own way of living. But to this tolerance of other people's manners and customs we must add daily practice in settling differences and disputes through the conference method, so that to the disposition to recognize differences as legitimate we add practice in the adjustment of rival claims on behalf of a concern for all interests represented in an area of conflict. Where this two-fold procedure is persisted in year in and year out there is some basis for hope that children will strive as adults for the appropriate means with which to preserve both domestic and international peace.

The pertinent principles of a changing society can emerge in children's minds as an outcome of class discussions. The teacher who is sensitive to the relation of social welfare to private advantage can utilize the issues arising out of classroom materials and the incidents of school life for the purpose of confronting boys and girls with the implications of this conflict. Here, too, he will teach his lesson best if he guides discussion ever with an eye to the neglected aspects in the argument as against pushing his own views to the fore. And where these neglected aspects are illustrations of fundamental principles of human relationships, students, under the teachers' guidance, will come in time to embody them in the structure of their thinking.

The significance of the life of the school in furthering basic principles of conduct has received too little attention. So, too, discussions on the relation of the school to the social order tend to center so exclusively upon indoctrinating children in the characteristics of a planned society that the *essentials for transition* to the living arrangements of tomorrow are permitted to lie fallow. For be it observed, the society of tomorrow, for which we would educate the young, is none other than the *trends in the present* with which they must identify their lives.

That is to say the social order with which teachers and parents must deal and for which they must prepare young people is much more concrete and specific and much nearer home than what ordinarily passes for the plans of a new social order. It pertains to the *immediate* and *remote results* in children's lives of the impact upon them of the influences and forces and conditions of modern living. To cope effectively with these outcomes is a far more complicated task than most discussions on educating for the world of tomorrow would seem to suggest.

We can only remark that almost entirely for the very young child and to a considerable degree for the adolescent, it becomes a matter of organizing school experiences and courses of study with an eye to remedying characteristic undernourishments. We refer to the undernourishments, for example, that result from inadequate participation in the basic processes of living; or from the absence of abiding relations with adults whom young people admire and respect; from contemporary exaggerated emphasis upon economic and materialistic values with its stunting of avenues of expression which human beings have always found health-giving; from difficulties in the way of socialization now that old forms of neighborliness are gone and obvious and direct opportunities for service no longer exist; from the impediments that beset young people seeking an understanding and an interpretation of their experiences in a literature and a philosophy couched in the language and reflecting the thought patterns of a pre-industrial civilization.

In the elementary school period these inadequacies necessitate providing experiences designed to build confidence and security in a naturally insecure world. They determine the character and the quality of the contacts we will help children to make with the institutions and the agencies of the community outside the school. They point to the necessity of acquainting children with what progress mankind has made, and helping them to derive therefrom a faith in the possibilities of men and women to continue rough hewing, as they have always done, significant values, beauty, and promise out of man's existence. Finally, they suggest the importance of opportunities for service to others in school and out, so that children may acquire thereby the sense of security that comes from fulfilling a function indispensable to others.

Not until he is well along in the secondary school will the student need to confront controversial issues in their raw and stark reality. Even here, he is entitled to assistance in maintaining balance and proportion and perspective. Above all, he will need to learn that the conflicts dividing men are commonly of a nature in which good and bad, right and wrong are sadly intertwined and are with difficulty distinguished. Consequently he will come to welcome the method of science as a tool for weighing evidence and sifting out the values involved in a knotty problem. To the extent that his previous experiences in school and home have equipped him with working principles of value, will he accord adequate weight to the considerations revealed by a thoughtful and unbiased analysis.

The method suggested differs both from indoctrination, as ordinarily interpreted, and the lack of direction and guidance usually implied in educating for the open mind. It assumes a definite responsibility to guide the thought and the behavior of young people in socially desirable directions, but it would exercise this influence in an educative manner. That is to say, it furthers intelligent appraisal and critical scrutiny of the principles it fosters in the process of their application so that at the proper time and a later stage in the individual's development these selfsame principles may become at once subject of study and objects of reconstruction, refinement, and revision. Education of this character prepares for a changing future without dogmatism or rigidity. It conceives of the school as perpetuating in American life the open road and new opportunities for fulfillment which constitute our richest inheritance from the American frontier.

Let us attempt to apply the principles we have discussed to the issues raised by attempts of totalitarian groups to use our free schools as means for undermining free government.

CHAPTER IX

Should Communists and Fascists Teach in the Schools?

THE past few years have imposed a heavy burden upon conscientious liberals. Traditionally they have contended for complete freedom of thought and expression in the public forum and unrestricted freedom of teaching in the classroom. "Ye shall know the truth and the truth shall make ye free," has been a sacred dictum.

A number of reasons prompts the liberal to ground his faith in the peaceful processes of persuasion as the only sound method for instituting changes in men's minds and subsequently in men's ways. First, he attributes to man a faculty of reason that enables him to appraise events and issues objectively and thus to determine the true interests of the individual and society. Untrammeled reason presupposes, secondly, a free flow of ideas, an open channel to the truth. This the liberal identifies with free competition in ideas. Sound public policy thus commits society to a deliberative procedure identical with that employed by an intelligent individual in his individual search for truth. And in time of tension and stress he turns for assurance to those inspiring words of Justice Holmes:

But when men have realized that time has upset many fighting faiths, they may come to believe even more than they believe the very foundations of their own conduct that the ultimate good desired is better reached by free trade in ideas—that the best test of truth is the power of the thought to get itself accepted in the competition of the market, and that truth is the only ground upon which their wishes safely can be carried out. That, at any rate, is the theory of our Constitution. It is an experiment as all life is an experiment. Every year if not every day we have to wager our salvation upon some prophecy based upon imperfect knowledge. While that experiment is part of our system I think we should be eternally vigilant against attempts to check the expression of opinions that we loathe and believe to be fraught with death, unless they so imminently threaten immediate interference with the lawful and pressing purposes of the law that an immediate check is required to save the country.

Finally the liberal believes our schools and colleges are society's most appropriate instruments for effecting constructive changes in the future. They acquaint the student with his cultural heritage, but not for the purpose of habituating him to the grooves in which his ancestors have moved; rather the past is used to emancipate him from the present and to serve as a point of reference from which to confront a novel future. Consequently student and teacher alike owe allegiance to more than the past or, for that matter, to the contemporary. Their concern is with the quality of living in the tomorrow. Toward this end they must be freed from the control of all interested groups. Particularly is it the teacher's function to instruct his students so that as a matter of habit they can arrive at undictated conclusions on controversial issues. The responsibility of the teacher thus centers primarily upon instruction in the methods of self-directed inquiry, not upon inculcating belief in any final set of dogmas.

These are the tenets of liberalism and of a liberal education. And, be it observed, the victories thus far won have been wrested primarily from conservatives who have placed the status quo above the emancipation of the individual from restrictions of class, of privileged group, and of government.

In recent years, however, the liberal's difficulties have come increasingly from the "left." For example, he sees the rights of a minority used not to extend further the scope of democratic living, but to "soften up" this society, and to sow the seeds of a discord designed to eventuate in dictatorship. These tactics are employed by fascists and communists alike.

They demand the right of freedom of assembly in order to hold meetings at which dissenters are howled down, and opponents maltreated. They claim the democratic privileges of speaking, of writing, and even of teaching, not for the sake of spreading the truth but in order to insinuate ideas that undermine faith in democratic processes.

All this confounds the liberal. He is aware that an attack upon these new enemies of free education may give aid and comfort to groups only too ready to cleanse the schools of "subversive" elements.

Naturally he hesitates to pull the chestnuts out of the fire for the conservatives; but neither can he in easy conscience sign a suicide pact with the enemies of a free society.

Perhaps a means of escape will suggest itself if we reexamine the tenets of traditional liberalism.

II

1. *First, to what extent is the doctrine of laissez faire in ideas applicable to education?*

Traditionally, as we have seen, the liberal draws an analogy between free competition in economic life and free competition in ideas. As the first is designed to promote invention, to lower prices, to stimulate efficiency, so the latter is assumed to reveal the truth that will make men free. And just as government control and restraint over trade were once thought to hamper and restrict business operations, so restraint upon the exercise of reason is believed to retard and corrupt the search for truth.

The applications of this theory to education are obvious. At his best the teacher can have no commitments to specific truths. Or if he harbors convictions on mooted questions, he will do no more than lay his views before his students as so much raw material for their own thinking.

How does this square with the realities of the present situation in school and college?

In the first place it *assumes the settled existence of the kind of society in which free inquiry can proceed unmolested.* It is conditioned upon the common acceptance and operation of values which constitute the groundwork of a free society. Only when these values are securely rooted in the confirmed ways in which citizens habitually think, feel, and act, can a liberal education truly function.

But it is precisely this fact that we commonly ignore. The sustaining structure of a liberal education we tend to take for granted. And while in times of peace and security a full consciousness of the supporting structure of a free education can perhaps be neglected with impunity, it is no longer a safe policy to pursue. The ideals and the working principles of a democratic education, if they are to survive in the world of today, must be taught, in the sense of habits acquired and principles of living consciously formulated. New needs give rise to new obligations.

It is quite important, however, to observe what is meant by developing democratic attitudes in the personality structures of boys and girls, since the description of democratic education thus far given applies to ways in which socially mature adults ideally function in their attempts to resolve situations of conflict and confusion and not to *the processes of education* prior to the young person's attainment of the age of intellectual and moral discretion. To attain to this stage it is necessary for the individual to subject himself to a period of careful tutelage.

What are the essentials of this tutelage?

One is that adults—by which we mean parents and teachers —shall give careful attention to the cultural and personality needs of children in the process of their growing up. Primary is the sense of security that comes from an emotional identification with family and community patterns of belief and conduct. The child begins life, not as a reasoning animal, but as an emotional and feeling being. His early emotional experiences furnish him with a first-hand knowledge of the world and of people and incorporate within him the fundamental feeling tones that will later characterize his attitudes toward his fellows. In order that these attitudes may be those of assurance and confidence he must feel that he belongs to the group in which he was born and in which he now lives. This means that teachers and parents and other educative agencies within the community are charged with the responsibility of building constructive rather than destructive attitudes in the young. As to the primary and elementary school, it suggests the use of the arts and crafts, drama, story and actual working projects which will help the child to identify himself with the ongoing life of his community.

At the same time the teacher must seek to relate the local family or group culture to the basic values of the larger community. The child of the foreign born must be helped to become an American; the children of rich and poor should learn to know each other, and share in common attitudes toward life that overarch in importance differences in economic and social class.

Nor does this imply a plan of instruction which stresses only uncritical satisfaction with the world as it is. It does, however, encourage emphasis upon the hopeful methods employed by people to obviate the evils that so plainly exist. It is designed to give one a sense of belonging to the group he has in mind to reform, much as he retains membership in his family while seeking to mend its ways. Indeed one function of the teacher in the elementary and the junior high school period is to sow the seeds of emancipation from local prejudices, to foster an acceptance of change, and to promote a readiness to envisage and to labor for a world different from that in which the individual is born. But this readiness to alter and to transform old ways, if it is to be healthily grounded, must be rooted in a conviction of membership in and a fundamental identification with the ways of the culture in which a person lives and moves and has his being.

How this may be brought about is, of course, a problem

in educational method. Particularly does it imply using for educational ends the child's normally friendly interest in the different. For the present it is sufficient to observe that this provision for the child to enter a world somewhat different from that in which he and his parents now dwell can and should be made without cultivating seeds of discord between him and his parents or a lack of confidence in the major characteristics and values of his society.

When the primary and the elementary school have given to the child an abiding assurance of membership in his society and a friendly disposition towards ways of living that differ from his own, the secondary school is ready to introduce him to responsible and controlled methods for instituting change. For secondary education corresponds roughly with a period in which young people are seeking to formulate their own ideals and codes of behavior—to reach out beyond family and immediate locality toward patterns of behavior that will give character and substance to their own lives. In the early years it is a period of hero worship in which children embody in tangible and visible personal form their aspirations; later these ideals assume a more abstract and general character. It is a period in which society's ills suggest an overly simple solution through the application of one large general formula.

The wise teacher will give heed to these adolescent characteristics. This is the time to introduce the student to the basic ideals of his own society and to develop *methods of thinking* by means of which he can attain the disciplined self-direction of adulthood.

Particularly is it important at this stage for teachers to distinguish between leading students to adopt foreordained conclusions on controversial questions and helping them to employ the major premises which they can use in the selection and rejection of data and in the final adoption of a conclusion. The liberal teacher, in his desire not to indoctrinate, has too often assumed that in some mysterious way facts will classify themselves. Consequently he has failed to help his students to distinguish between the facts in a given situation and the *values* by means of which these same facts are weighed for a sound conclusion.

Herein, for example, lies the difference between the obligations of a science teacher and a teacher whose subject matter relates to political, social, or economic behavior. For the scientist no major premises or fundamental hypotheses are sacred. At best they are temporary resting points in an endless search for further knowledge regarding the phenomena and behavior of nature. But within the field of social behavior and man's relations to man, values, basic assumptions of living, constitute the major premises by reference to which inquiry checks on the relevance of its data and the appropriateness of its conclusions. Do we question, for example, the validity of public relief as against private philanthropy; or the relative advantage of old age pensions as against the institutional care of the helpless aged? We search out the data which sheds light upon the effect of the one or the other on the individuals affected. That is, we *assume* that the method which most adequately enhances or safeguards the worth of personality is the more appropriate method, since the worth of personality is a fundamental principle from which in a democratic society reasoning starts and to which it returns.

The moral for our present purpose is that a teacher—as a condition of professional fitness—must help his students to acquire and use those basic principles of thought and action which constitute the groundwork of democratic thinking and action. He recognizes that one and the same principle may lead his students to differ as to conclusions and prompt him perhaps to differ from them. If this difference is an honest one, he need have no concern. But he must bestir himself to see that differing conclusions trace back to the fundamental axioms of thought that underlie a free society.

Consequently, again, there is no place in the secondary school for a teacher who subordinates his professional responsibility to an authority alien to the educational needs of his students.

But someone will inquire, "Are the assumptions that constitute the framework of a democratic society nowhere to be challenged in education? Are they absolutes before which student and teacher must prostrate themselves; theirs to do and die but not to reason why?"

Not at all. But once the question of the appropriateness or the validity of basic principles arises, we have, in a sense, passed to a third stage in an individual's education, to the stage of higher education.[1] At this point as in the forum of public opinion generally, there should be no restrictions or limitations upon a *scholarly* and *unbiased* search for truth.

But, we repeat, a scholarly and unbiased search for truth! There is no identity between an untrammeled pursuit of truth and propaganda; and while a college instructor's earnest convictions on a specific question or with respect to a fundamental principle under investigation can freely be expressed, this in no way sanctions the control and sorting of information for his own ends or a selection of evidence for the purpose of tipping the scales in favor of one view as against another.

Thus at each stage in the education of his students a teacher must subordinate himself to *a professional discipline*. In the early years of education this discipline requires that he promote the child's sense of membership within a family, a racial, political, cultural group and, at one and the same time, lay the foundations for a healthy emancipation from provincialism. On the secondary level of education it implies the constructive introduction of the student to the fundamental values that permeate the society of which he is a member; and it calls for skill in teaching students how to employ the

[1] It is not intended here to identify these stages in development strictly with the present administrative divisions of secondary and higher education.

methods of thinking and inquiry which condition an adequate realization of these values. In college and graduate school this discipline requires allegiance to the methods of thinking and research characteristic of and peculiar to an unbiased search for truth. While it sanctions the examination and the appraisal of any and all values by which men live, it precludes propaganda. As the Graduate Faculty of Political and Social Science of the New School for Social Research have said, it requires "that no member of the Faculty can be a member of any political group which asserts the right to dictate in matters of science or scientific opinion."

III

Liberals have insisted that teaching in no way deprives a teacher of his prerogatives as a citizen. Have we offended against this principle? Have we not set up qualifications and requirements which run counter to a teacher's right as a citizen to arrive at undictated conclusions, to state his ideas with impunity and to affiliate himself with organizations and movements designed to convince other citizens of the truth as he sees it?

Doubtless this question was more easily answered when elementary and secondary schools interpreted their function as primarily purveyors of information and not chiefly as character building agents. It is simpler also if we believe that a teacher can function as a plural personality separating nicely his influence upon children within the classroom from the influence which may emanate from him by virtue of his interests and activities outside the classroom. As a plain matter of fact no personality can so divide itself. But the import of out-of-school influences upon teaching does vary with communities. Obviously the actions of a teacher in a large city where anonymity is easily acquired do not carry the same implications as in an isolated rural community. The same holds true of differences in the age levels of children with whom a teacher works. It would seem, therefore, that the vital question is not whether a teacher may or may not function as a citizen apart from his teaching, but rather what actions as citizen can be considered irrelevant to the satisfactory performance of his duties as a teacher? This question can only be answered in the light of a specific situation and a specific community. It is sufficient for us to emphasize that no conscientious teacher can ignore the fact that there is some relationship between his life outside school and his influence within the classroom.

More pertinent is the recent tendency to insist, not that the teacher as a citizen has rights as such, but that the teacher's rights as a teacher are identical with his rights *as a citizen*. Consequently, it is assumed, that since the teacher as a citizen has the right to express his private views and to win converts to them, this remains his right as a teacher and to deny him the privilege of its exercise in the classroom is to infringe upon his academic freedom.

But surely there is a difference. One is a citizen by virtue of his birth or his residence in a given locality, factors over which he may have little control. Since, however, a free society wishes its members to function as contributing agents, the civil rights of freedom of assembly, of the press, and of thought and expression are guaranteed.

Membership in a professional organization is of a different order. Membership in a school faculty is membership within a voluntary organization and quite properly carries with it the assumption of a dedication to specific purposes and a professional discipline. Hence general acceptance of, or agreement with, the purposes of the school may properly be required as a condition of membership in a faculty and loyalty to its purposes a condition of continued membership.

Now public schools and colleges are established for the purpose of preparing young people for effective participation in democratic citizenship, within the framework of the Constitution of the state and the nation and the laws of the country. Loyalty and obedience to these can appropriately be exacted. And while liberals object quite properly to the signing of a loyalty oath, on both psychological and methodological grounds, it must not be inferred that in so doing they object to the requirement of loyalty to the government as such or to the fundamental principles and ideals of the school system which teachers undertake to serve.

It follows that conduct becoming a teacher cannot rightfully include membership in any group or organization or party dedicated to a policy of undermining the essential structure of our government or our way of life. Or of instilling convictions and beliefs in children or young people toward this end. Or of deliberately organizing materials of learning and classroom experience that subordinate students to the ends of the teacher or to the purposes of an outside group; in short, that fails to see in the student an educational end in himself.

Nor do these restrictions constitute an infringement upon academic freedom. Once more, we repeat, academic freedom is not synonymous with the freedom to use students for ulterior purposes. Academic freedom is rather the privilege to follow the procedures of democratic learning; to be free from influences such as the power interests sought some years ago to exercise in the writing of text books, or the Communist Party has recently exerted upon the teachers subject to its control.

Nor, again, do these restrictions infringe upon a teacher's right as a citizen. Common honesty requires of a teacher in the public schools, who sincerely believes that a totalitarian form of government should replace our democratic and representative form of government, that he resign his position. As a citizen, unhampered by professional discipline, he can exercise his freedom to write and speak or otherwise to engage in lawful efforts to transform his government.

From this analysis it is relatively simple to define our attitude toward communists and fascists in our schools, or to weigh the appropriateness of teachers becoming members of any organization that subordinates professional performance to its own ends. In each case it is not a belief in communism or fascism as such that renders membership improper. It is rather the evidence at hand, beyond a reasonable doubt, that communist and fascist party discipline conflicts with and subordinates to its own ends the professional discipline of teaching.

But, it may be asked, "Is not the Communist Party legally recognized? Do not the names of candidates for office on the Communist ticket appear legally upon the party ballot in a number of states for whom anyone may legally vote? Are we not therefore conditioning the right to teach upon the forfeiture of legal rights? Once teachers are denied the right to belong to a Communist or a Fascist Party, will not similar rules be applied to Socialists in communities where Socialists are unpopular and to Republicans or Democrats where the latter are in disfavor?"

To which we reply that the analogy is not valid. There is evidence that Communist and Fascist party discipline is unique and is not at all similar to that exercised by other parties.

The Communist Party, in the area to which we refer (and doubtless Fascist groups as well) has secretly controlled the activities of its members for purposes that can properly be termed subversive. A political party, in any respectable meaning of the term political, does not require its members to falsify the fact of their membership. Nor does it expect its members to perjure themselves rather than to testify against another member; or insist, as a matter of principle, that they place the interests of party before the interests of the state; or engage in conduct designed cleverly to undermine civil order, and to loosen the cement of honest and open relations between men. Unfortunately, there is evidence not only of behavior of precisely this character on the part of communist teachers in our schools, but, as well, that this behavior has conformed to the secret instruction of party agents.

Consider, for example, the following instructions to teachers that appeared in *The Communist* in May, 1937:

. . . the Party must take careful steps to see that all teacher comrades are given thorough education in the teaching of Marxism-Leninism. Only when teachers have really mastered Marxism-Leninism will they be able skillfully to inject it into their teaching at the least risk of exposure and at the same time to conduct struggles around the schools in a truly Bolshevik manner.

Surely we have not only the right but the obligation, when there is evidence of this type of control over teaching, to insist that our teachers, like Caesar's wife, be above suspicion!

But what becomes of the principle that teachers be judged on the basis of their conduct as individuals and not on belief?

We reply that this principle still holds good. May we make our position clear, since it relates to certain reservations and safeguards regarding membership in Communist groups upon which liberals will have to insist.

For example, there are good reasons why a community, when it institutes regulations with respect to non-membership in the Communist Party, should impose no *ex post facto* penalties. Indeed, this is a sound principle to employ with respect to all prohibitions. But in the present instance it is peculiarly important since many individuals, who were once communist in their sympathies and who joined the party out of loyalty to what seemed to them genuinely democratic principles at work in the Russian experiment, have come to view their actions in quite a different light. The essential is to judge as best we can the motives and the intentions of the individual as distinct from what we may consider to be the validity of his conclusions. Since, however, there is evidence that the conduct of the Party and its control over members is anti-democratic and subversive in its discipline, there is just ground for requiring non-membership as a condition for induction into teaching and as a condition for continued service as a teacher.

By applying these regulations to the future rather than

to the past no injury will be done to those who once affiliated themselves with communism through democratic motives. And, on the other hand, these restrictions tend to insure that from a given day forth membership in the Party will constitute conduct unbecoming a teacher.

IV

There remains something to be said regarding the necessary safeguards to provide with respect to charges of conduct unbecoming a teacher, particularly when these relate to so-called subversive teaching.

These are times which try men's souls and, in periods of storm and stress, the teacher's task is a hard one. Hysteria on the right and hysteria on the left easily arouse witch-hunting proclivities. Nor are groups lacking that are all too ready to use any opportunity to becloud issues; to damn as subversive and dangerous views with which they disagree or that run counter to their selfish interests.

For this reason every precaution should be taken to insure competent and professional judgment upon the conduct of any teacher who may be charged with abusing his privileges as a teacher. Trial by a jury consisting, in part, at least, of those who are his peers would seem to be a minimum essential.

Nor should any teacher be condemned on the basis of an isolated incident. Mistakes of judgment are easily made. The excitement or the enthusiasm of the moment in a class discussion can easily result in an error which should be recognized only for what it is, a single mistake. A professionally competent judgment on a teacher's work will distinguish between one incident and the general trend and character of his work. Persistent and habitual efforts to mould the minds of students in the direction of a teacher's will or in a manner injurious to their healthy growth is a much safer criterion to employ than an isolated case of error or bad judgment.

And may we suggest also that a jury of one's peers is not of necessity adequate protection for a teacher on trial in a period of emotional excitement. It is by no means true that faculty members are more democratic, or unbiased or less easily swayed than an administrator. For this reason to a jury consisting of faculty members might safely be added not only administrative officers and laymen but probably competent individuals from outside the locality affected.

We return, in conclusion, to the liberal's dilemma with which we began. We mentioned his fear that in meeting the menace of totalitarian radicalism he would give aid and comfort to the conservative forces against whom he has waged the traditional battles of freedom. But neither can he afford to condone conduct from any source that offends against the integrity of the individual, or the growing personality of the child. In these days particularly he cannot with honesty condone the behavior of Communists and Fascists similar in principle to what he has long opposed in the conservative. The conditions of his effectiveness are one with the purity of the teaching for which he strives. He must insist that the hands of all who deal with children be clean!

CHAPTER X

Schools for Schooling vs. Schools for Education

MODERN trends in education can be understood best by observing that schools for schooling are striving to become schools for education. Historically, the school is a supplementary institution. It originated out of the efforts of people to realize cooperatively certain essentials in the education of children that parents could not realize individually. The modern school still defines its task in this context. It seeks deliberately to supplement and reinforce and, on occasion, to offset influences in the community that bear upon young people. The difference between the traditional and the modern school thus turns upon the way in which each conceives this supplementary function.

Generations ago, the accepted task of the school was to introduce children to books and to the skills essential for reading, writing and figuring. These skills were basic for economic well-being as well as for enabling the individual to read and interpret the Bible for himself, and thus to point the way to salvation. Book knowledge supplemented rich, if not varied, experiences that children and adolescents acquired normally in the home, the church, the town meeting and other community enterprises. Books alone were scarce. There were no public libraries and while a few fortunate individuals accumulated treasuries of their own, few possessed the skill or the resources with which to instruct the young.

Today books and academic education are still important. Indeed more important than yesterday, since we live in a civilization that is increasingly dependent upon the arts of verbal communication. Moreover, the fact that by and large children are introduced to processes and to concepts at an extremely early age (earlier by far than was common in the old days) and that the level of general education for the mass of people is being steadily raised, complicates the professional task of the teacher. He must cope with two contradictory factors. Children are younger than they once were and they attend school longer; but experiences outside of school that should give body and substance to what they are learning are increasingly inadequate. They enter school deficient in first-hand contact with life, lacking the primary matrix out of which to develop both the working habits and the working ideas essential for understanding and mastering their world. There is need to supplement this impoverished environment, if learning is to be vital.

Consider, for example, the more obvious changes in home life and their possible implications for the school. How many children today are privileged to know at first hand the nature of their father's occupation? Or to help him with the work so important for the family's well being? Or, for that matter, to share with the father in recreational activities? Play, as well as work, takes place on horizontal age lines rather than vertical, with the result that children are deprived of intimate relations with the father of the family, and the father finds it difficult, if not impossible, to communicate freely with his children; to live fruitfully in their lives.

To the defective role of the father we must add, a growing tendency toward a similar abdication of the mother's function. In many homes the mother, as well as the father, engages in vocational and non-vocational activities which take her out of the home. Modern life, thus, seems to conspire against children. Fewer and fewer are the occasions for them to share with their elders in rich and varied activities essential for the family's well being.

Changes of this character suggest a new supplementary role for the school. Perhaps men teachers in the elementary grades can offset in part the limited role of the father. The absence of genuine tasks in the home for children to perform, their remoteness from the processes involved in providing food, clothing, and shelter, suggest provision for first-hand participation in school activities. This validates in many communities the school luncheon, not merely to insure an adequate noon-day meal but to enable children at various age levels to learn about the selection, preparation, and the serving of food. Older children can assume a responsibility for serving the younger and, in the process, acquire both a practical knowledge of the principles of nutrition and a sympathetic understanding of the needs and the characteristics of younger boys and girls, with resulting beneficial effects upon the relations of younger and older children in the home.

These new procedures in no way imply that the modern school seeks to replace the home. Obviously this is impossible. Psychological studies of childhood and youth emphasize the potent influence upon a child's personality of relationships within the family even in comparatively vacant homes. All that the school can hope to do is to offset certain limitations inherent in modern conditions of living.

Once we grant the school should function as a cooperative agency to meet the developmental needs of boys and girls, it follows that its task in each community will vary with local needs and local resources in materials and personnel. Communities differ. The small town in a rural district is less regimented in its living arrangements than a suburban area inhabited largely by a commuting or an apartment dwelling population. Consequently the specific needs of children and the specific measures a school should undertake in order to meet these needs also differ. In each case, however, the school and the community will guarantee to each child certain essential conditions as a preliminary to a good education.

For example, we cannot train vigorous and healthy minds without reference to the factors that make for healthy bodies and healthy emotional dispositions. In theory few will question the importance of physical health as a pre-condition of good schooling. Actually, this first essential in education is by no means guaranteed to all children. Altogether too many are neglected physically despite the fact that we know the hazards of permitting young people to grow up undernourished in body. Let us not forget that the most devoted followers of Hitler in Germany sprang from a generation starved and dwarfed in body and in mind, victims of the last war and the blockade which the allies imposed upon a defeated people after the signing of the Armistice. Nazi Germany testifies to the moral effects of undernourishment and starvation. But America, too, has its danger zones. It is no accident that crime waves, intolerance, and racial antagonism flourish in poverty stricken neighborhoods inhabited by children who are ill-housed, ill-fed, and physically neglected.

So, too, there are emotional conditions of good health. Emotional factors in growth require renewed emphasis at a time when we are repeatedly assured that the crisis of our times will be cured only when schools and colleges concentrate exclusively "upon the intellectual training of the young."

To be sure, the task of the school includes the training of the mind, but if we would have a well trained and well disciplined mind function effectively, we cannot neglect the soil in which it grows. In recent years the research and practice of mental hygiene have made clear the necessary ingredients of this soil, the primary conditions of the "life of reason." We say *primary* conditions because, in a very real sense, the extent to which emotional needs are met prior to the age of schooling affect directly what a child will make of himself in school; whether he will stumble and fail or proceed normally and creatively. Moreover, these primary necessities are *continuing* conditions. They are needs which all, adults as well as young, must satisfy in order to live happily and fruitfully with their fellows.

II

First of these needs is an assurance of achievement.

It is commonly remarked that the child of some years ago was a genuine member of the family in that he could pull an oar in the common cause. Tasks beckoned in sufficient numbers to give him a sense of shared membership in the home. Not infrequently educators bemoan the passing of the period in which children were economic assets to the family.

This transformation in the child's status is not altogether bad. The work thrust upon children in the pioneer home, as on many a poverty stricken tenant's farm of today, was not in all respects healthy. The backs of children, as well as their spirits, were often broken by work. In contrast with this exploitation of children, the recognition of childhood as a unique and distinctive stage of growth is a godsend. The fact that children can no longer fit into the adult scheme of work has led to the discovery of distinctive characteristics peculiar to childhood.

As so often happens, however, the pendulum has swung too far. Few children now sense at first-hand tangible and irrefutable evidence of being needed, or of exercising an indispensable function in the family circle. Nor do they encounter conditions in the home designed to build habits of responsibility, a faithfulness to regular tasks, the performance of which affect directly and obviously the lives of others. Indeed it was John Dewey's observation of this gradual elimination of opportunities from the lives of young people that led him some fifty years ago, to conceive the ideal school on the pattern of the ideal home. Said he,

The child participates in the household occupations, and thereby gets habits of industry, order, and regard for the rights and ideas of others, and the fundamental habit of subordinating his activities to the general interest of the household. Participation in these household tasks becomes an opportunity for gaining knowledge. The ideal home would naturally have a workshop where the child could work out his constructive instincts. It would have a miniature laboratory to which his inquiries could be directed. The life of the child would extend out-of-doors to the garden, the surrounding fields and forest. He would have his excursions, his walks and talks, which the larger world out-of-doors would open to him.

Now if we organize and generalize all of this, we have the ideal school.[1]

The need to achieve is more than a private and individualistic urge. It has its roots in the lives of others. It is social as well as private and personal in its origin and in its healthy expression. In recent years progressive educators have busily explored the child's need for achievement as one aspect of self-expression, and progressive teachers have devised ingenious ways of helping the child to express his nature through unique and distinctive activities. Frequently, however, they have neglected the equally important task of fusing self-expressive behavior and creative living in the lives of others.

To foster this more comprehensive expression, a continuous and graded series of activities or experiences is necessary. By this we do not mean specific activities analogous to the prescribed lessons of a text book. Rather do we envisage the careful planning of school projects that enable young people, from kindergarten through college, to merge self-expressive and socially valuable behavior.

Teachers and parents can foresee some types of activities calculated to lay the basis for socially sensitive growth. But not all, since the manner in which experiences affect the inner lives of children is as significant as the activities themselves. The method of guidance is of equal importance with the occasions used.

The war has created opportunities for cooperative activities not so evident prior to the war. The initial step was taken, in many instances, when air-raid precautions became imperative. But many schools have gone far beyond emer-

[1] *The School and Society*, p. 52. Chicago: University of Chicago Press, 1900.

gency provisions in which the older children served as wardens, planned games, and provided interesting diversions for the younger children during the long tense moments of an air-raid drill. The plain necessity of keeping buildings clean and otherwise supplementing the work of janitors and cleaners, involves work that cannot be gainsaid.

In one elementary school, the older children have undertaken to assist in the care of younger children during rest periods and meal hours. In addition, they help to care for rooms, build furniture and equipment for the kindergarten, and devote art periods to the illustration of stories and nursery rhymes for the very young. Out of this has come not merely an intimate acquaintance between age groups, a fellowship, or better, a family atmosphere hitherto absent in the school, but as well a stabilizing emotional influence upon the older children themselves. The work of the school is no less interesting. The child with an art, a shop, or a science or food interest can still use this interest to better his knowledge and his skill; but, more, he grounds it firmly and gives it objective validity by virtue of the fact that by means of it he furthers the life of his community. To the surprise of the shop teachers in this institution, the sixth grade boys, who devoted their shop periods to the construction of furniture for the kindergarten, were not only as keenly interested in their work as formerly, but they more willingly held themselves to a high level of performance. They employed an effective and objective standard for good work and were freed from the temptation to conclude at a critical moment "Well, anyway, that is good enough for me."

Of chief importance, in this instance, is the quality of relationships fostered by these new departures. The older children no longer look upon the very young child as a nuisance and a pest. Nor is the older child an indifferent or an unsympathetic stranger to the young. A good family atmosphere pervades the school and genuine affection has grown up between big and little. Moreover, service experiences yield

grist for discussions on the part of older children in which
the behavior traits of the small child are made known and
thus, indirectly, the older .children acquire an insight into
their own behavior in relation to their brothers and sisters.
Parents report less tension and improved relationships within
their homes.

A similar program can extend into the high school, but,
as we approach adolescence, and certainly the upper years
of high school, it is all important for the young person to
reach out into the larger community by means of well-established and more fully defined interests. Thus the art student,
as an integral part of his development as an artist, can study
and perhaps contribute toward meeting the art needs of the
community. Similarly the science student can assist in a hospital or a health clinic or perhaps in a municipal health department where scientific principles receive application. He
thus acquires a sense of reality not otherwise possible and
the numerous possibilities of science as a vocational and a
civic contribution become manifest to him.

Recently a class group in a secondary school conducted a
survey of the immediate community in which the school is
located. In the course of their investigation they discovered
a number of mothers of poor families who were unable to
supplement the family income because of the need to remain
home with their children. After deliberating upon the situation, the class decided to appeal to the student body in support of the establishment of a day nursery. The girls volun-
teered to assist a trained worker in the nursery, and to acquire the essentials of child care thus involved; other students
helped to equip it. In short, out of a classroom study, blos-
somed a social-civic project which gave first-hand assurance
to the students that they could play a significant role in their
community along the lines of a major interest of the school.

It is thus that the school can provide what the home of
yesterday once provided, an opportunity to employ one's
talents in ways that young and old alike recognize as signifi-

cant. Healthy progress into adulthood requires open channels of expression for these normal tendencies of youth.

This suggests that education on the secondary and college levels should establish a close relationship between the well defined interests and abilities of young people and economic, social, and civic life. When it is possible to give a job reference to these interests and abilities, well and good; particularly for boys and girls who for one reason or another cannot or should not remain in school. But the relating of a student's interests and capabilities to the "world of affairs" should not be limited to their economic and vocational applications. It is a fair criticism of both professional and vocational education, that they neglect the social-civic and cultural implications of the vocational function. By and large these implications have been subordinated to an emphasis upon personal economic success. Practical reasons, as well as theoretical, suggest today a more generous exploitation of the student's interest. In so far as young people are called upon to adjust themselves to a period of prolonged non-employment in economic life, it is important that they discover attractive opportunities for service to the community along lines they can sense as relevant.

Possibilities of this nature are nearer at hand than we have thought. Many libraries, museums, and institutions of applied art and science have added to their service functions educational activities involving children and youth. Nor are these developments restricted to matters of passive interest alone. Under the influence of the new education they take on an active character. What libraries, museums and an occasional research institution have initiated in a small way, departments of municipal, county, and state governments can develop as an integral part of their normal functioning. At present these departments of government tend to limit their activities to the performance of direct services. We suggest that they add, better that they integrate, the educational and the service function. A two-fold contribution might ensue. Young people would encounter opportunities for public service while in the process of continuing their education; and governmental departments, by virtue of their new educational responsibilities, might well become permeated with a sadly needed spirit of service.

The summer work camp movement can also contribute to the year-round school and college program. Each year for some years work camps have enrolled an increasing number of young people who, often without wage or salary, devote their summers to physical labor upon projects clearly needed by a community or a social agency. These young people engage in work such as clearing land, remodeling or erecting buildings, constructing an irrigation project, roadmaking and, more recently, farm labor. In each instance they realize that the work they do meets a crucial need. Under these conditions work becomes more than an exchange of labor for money. It acquires an aesthetic and spiritual quality and fosters social maturity.

We stated a moment ago that the need for a sense of achievement comprises more than an individual urge; that it is social as well as individual in its constitution. Something remains to be said about the need for a sense of belonging as such and its educational importance for young people of today.

The assurance that one is accepted by others, that his position in a family or a group or a community is unquestioned, that his status is secure, is one of the prime essentials of mental health for individuals in childhood and adulthood alike. It conditions that inner confidence and self-respect so requisite for sane and balanced relations with our fellows. And just as the need for achievement includes in a measure this sense of belonging, so a healthy realization of belonging is furthered by the knowledge that others need us and are dependent upon us for the services we alone can render.

The full implications of this sense of belonging are myriad. The serious consequences of its absence are manifest in the maladjustments of the unwanted child who remains unaccepted emotionally by his parents. The difficulties frequently encountered by children of minority groups, the colored child in a school predominantly of whites who are hostile to racial equality, of the Jewish boy or girl striving to grow up in an anti-semitic community, and the distortions of behavior and attitude that result unless wisely counteracted by love and understanding in the home, illustrate the effects of emotional undernourishment in this area. Here again no dividing line separates the psychological from the social. Consequently the educator must remain sensitive to both sets of factors. On the one hand he will search the environment, life in home and community, for causes of undernourishment which reflect themselves in the behavior of young people and, on the other, he will utilize all resources available to offset these limitations through individual guidance and curriculum planning.

What are the limitations he encounters commonly in American life today?

One is lack of membership in a community, larger than the family, with well-defined common ideals and aspirations and known codes of behavior. Sometime ago Austin McCormick, formerly Commissioner of Corrections in New York City, gave as one explanation of delinquency in city children the fact of anonymity. A child who plays truant from school in a small town is aware of easy identification. In the large city, however, he has but to step out of the school building in order to lose himself in the crowd.

Many children encounter at an extremely early age a confusing competition of standards; the code of the home, the discipline of the school, and the expectations of the gang run counter to each other.

This suggests a relationship between school and home that will permit parents and teachers and children to create a genuine community of interests. The experiment of one settlement house in New York City, where parents take turns in assisting the teacher in charge of the nursery group, and thus learn at first-hand the essentials of children's diet and rest, how to direct play and to control behavior at various stages of development, may be prophetic of the future role of the school in relation to young parents.

Obviously parents are limited in their ability to engage in the activities of older children, but there is continued need for them to share in common enterprises in school and home and community. These common enterprises will have in mind several purposes: to provide objective occasions for young and old to work together with an eye toward mutual understanding and affection, to promote greater consistency in work habits and in methods of discipline as between home and school; and, in a period of cultural confusion, to enable parents and children and teachers to evolve consistent standards and ideals of behavior.

The new education can also help children and adolescents to achieve a satisfying status as children and as adolescents. Take the adolescent, for example. The tragedy of his situation during the depression derived from the fact that he lacked a well defined status. He was neither child nor adult. The steady lengthening of the period of non-participation in economic life undermined his self-respect. Consider, for instance, what happens to traditional characteristics of adolescence such as the youth's desire to establish a healthy independence of his parents; to form his own judgments and to regulate his own behavior; to establish new relationships with the opposite sex; to become self-sufficient economically. All of these presuppose for their realization conditions of living more typical of the past than of what lies ahead. Once the conditions requisite for their attainment undergo change, and they are changing, the dependence of the young upon parents is prolonged, childhood lengthens out and the adolescent tends to linger (albeit with resentment and impatience) upon the threshold of childhood rather than to venture hopefully into adulthood.

Does this enlarged conception of the task of the school mean that it will cease to function as a school? That intellectual and scholarly training will be subordinated to the development of the "whole child" and the "total personality"?

By no means. The procedure suggested is designed to better the intellectual output of the schools. Nothing in the new education need militate against the training of the mind. Indeed an intellectual tool is most efficiently mastered and employed when it is acquired under conditions that clearly indicate its relevance. As Elliott Smith once remarked, "a tool is as useful as the use made of it in its acquisition." We envisage, then, a relevant emphasis upon tools of learning, but a relevance that is evident to the young person while in the process of learning.

Once the essentials of readiness, that results from maturity, and a sense of relevance are assured schools can concentrate vigorously upon the intellectual development of their pupils. This requires, moreover, a wise selection of subject matter as well as skillful methods in stimulating creative inquiry, imagination, and thought. Our previous criticism of a curriculum of the great books was not intended to discourage the use of the classics with young people at the right time and of an appropriate kind. Let those who would be arbitrary in these matters take seriously Mark Van Doren's injunction that "there is no disciplinary value in a study that is not taught and learned with relish." Many of the neo-formalists neglect the importance of this fact of relish. Nor do we use the term lightly. We refer to the momentous fact of individual differences in background, experience, and talent. Those who would ride rough-shod over uniqueness and peculiar potentiality might recall with profit the words of that wise teacher, John Adams, who once remarked that the verb teach in the sentence "I teach John Latin" governs two accusatives. Perhaps a knowledge of the resources and the promise of John and of Latin in relation to each other will suggest a policy of non-intercourse; whereas similar information regarding Harry and Latin will encourage not merely an intimate acquaintance between the two but a strong attachment to Greek as well.

There is a necessary content out of the past to which schools should introduce their students—a content not to be selected and listed arbitrarily in school and college catalogue as a uniform and required curriculum for all, but chosen lovingly and fearfully by wise teachers who seek to marry the peculiar promise of the student and the rich resources of our culture. Material that constitutes an open sesame to life's values for one student may defy the most skillful teacher's efforts with another. And for a very good reason. Values as such reside in Greek or Latin or mathematics in the same manner only that indigestion dwells within cold mince pie. The individual in each case is an important contributing agent. Values require for their emergence a living interplay between a unique personality and an appropriate subject matter. Consequently there is no avoiding the necessity of selecting and adapting educative materials to groups and individuals. Indeed, it is precisely this selection and adaptation that define the genius as well as the profession of teaching.

Once this need for variation in method and content is recognized it is necessary to add that the arts of reading and of communication possess a peculiar significance today. No one can examine the characteristics of our civilization and discount the importance of book learning and verbal education. Words and abstract symbols acquire greater importance daily as instruments for effecting changes in men's ways. Moreover, physical proximity is less important than yesterday in promoting group thought and group action. More and more we fit our thoughts and our behavior into plans we hold in common with individuals and groups widely separated in space. Education, accordingly, must strive to equip young people to use and employ the instruments of an increasingly impersonal and verbal civilization. This means on the one hand that the school should provide training that renders people immune to the misuse of modern facilities for disseminating ideas and arousing emotion; on the other hand, it suggests that it take positive steps to equip young people with the techniques of cautious and controlled thinking. Each subject can serve this end by developing its unique method for gathering data, testing evidence, drawing conclusions. And each subject can contribute in its own way toward helping youth build a scheme of values characteristic of free men in a democratic society.

IV

American education has been handicapped for some years by a misapplication of the scientific spirit. Science in education, particularly on school and college levels, has discouraged all traffic in values, promoting instead an attitude of ethical neutrality on the issues of life. The assumption has been that once young people are encouraged to gather all the facts pertaining to a controversial question they can safely formulate their own conclusions. Evidently the values men employ in the weighing and the sifting of relevant data are to grow of their own accord.

Thus have American schools deprived young people of their birthright; for democracy is their spiritual inheritance. Only when the school succeeds in organizing ways of living within the school that both exemplify what men mean by democracy and acquaint young people with the long struggle of their ancestors to bring democracy into being, will it have satisfied still another need for healthy growth; the need for identification with an on-going tradition.

Two changes in our traditional ways of living explain the necessity today for a program of Americanization in harmony with democratic ideals.

In the first place the safety valve of the frontier and the

open road to economic success as once conceived no longer exist. The recent depression marked clearly a tendency, long evident to students of economics; a settling down economically, which precludes easy movement from one vocational effort to another. The dissatisfied or the failures can no longer pull up stakes in one locality or one vocation with the practical assurance of a successful "new deal" elsewhere. Groups which in the past have either changed their location under pressure, or caused others to yield to them in conflict, must learn to adjust differences and work out harmonious relations with others. If not, we shall enter an era of violence and aggression of a character already presaged by the intolerant behavior of our Black Legions, our Ku Klux Klans and more recent manifestations of self-constituted guardians of "Americanism."

Secondly, we can no longer assume that young people will grow naturally and normally into the practices and faith of democracy. On the contrary, there is evidence that the naive impulses of youth lend themselves readily to authoritarian creeds. We have in mind, for example, traits such as impatience with deliberative methods in the solution of critical problems; the tendency of youth to oversimplify a situation; his greater concern for the end, the goal, which he seeks than for the possibilities of growth and development contained within the means used for arriving at the goal; his proneness to cut through conventional procedure in order to secure speedy results; his ignorance of tradition and his natural indifference to lessons of the past. These are some of the characteristics of youth which explain in part events of recent years in Germany and Italy. Only thus can we account for the situation in which a German Reichstag voted away the rights of representative government acquired out of centuries of struggle.

These facts suggest that schools undertake more directly than heretofore a conscious introduction of our youth to the democratic tradition.

But is there common agreement upon the elements of this tradition, an acceptance of principles that can find exemplification in the total life of the school?

We believe there is. Indeed these principles are identical with those stressed in our previous discussion. They require translation only into the life of the school and the work of the classroom.

First is a dynamic conception of the worth of the individual; a respect and reverence for the integrity and the uniqueness of personality; an uncommon faith in the potentialities of the common man.

Apart from practicing what they preach (a first essential indeed!) there is much that schools can do to promote a conscious formulation of the principle that people are to be valued as people.

Each subject in the curriculum has a unique contribution to make toward enhancing the dignity of man. In the first place, history and the social studies can describe the gradual rise of the idea of man's worth, and the long tortuous path human beings have travelled in the process of its validation. So, too, the study of contemporary problems will illustrate the perennial struggle to keep this ideal alive and healthy, along with sickening examples of reversions to authority and dictatorship. Atavistic revivals of man's enslavement of men testify dramatically to the fact that centuries of painful advance can quickly be lost. History, too, with the help of literature and art and dramatic work can familiarize students with the contributions to our common culture from the racial groups that compose our variegated population, at the same time that it knits them in kinship to their fellows in loyalty to overarching ideals. And science may add authority to the hope that men will one day realize a society in which each person is appraised for what he is, irrespective of his race, or creed, or previous condition of servitude.

The school can likewise marshal positive forces on behalf of healthy personality development and in this process affirm the value of uniqueness. Toward this end each subject has its part to play. Traditionally, of course, the function of the arts and crafts is to further uniqueness and originality of expression. But other subjects will serve the cause by encouraging the development of special abilities and creative interests. Each field of work lends itself not alone to self-expressive activity but to a sensitive awareness and response to the thoughts and feelings of others.

Finally there is the life of the school as a whole, which can organize to exemplify and promote a regard for the individual and a friendly concern for conditions that give substance to this regard. Intellectually, as well as socially and economically and vocationally, a school includes boys and girls who are unlike. These unlikenesses can be used deliberately to develop an appreciation for a democracy of differences. When, for example, no gulf separates students who are perparing for different kinds of life work—college, art, business, vocations of hand and brain; or occasions are sought to engage young people of all economic classes and racial backgrounds in common tasks; and extra-curricular as well as classroom projects are used so that the different endowments and aptitudes of pupils further mutual understanding and respect rather than envy and hostility—then indeed does the school succeed in promoting the conception of worth. Morality of action is more effective than knowledge about morality, but more desirable still is a situation in which practice and theory reinforce each other.

A dynamic conception of the worth of individuals is the first element in the American tradition. The second relates to the method whereby conditions secure and maintain the expression and the development of potentialities. It is the principle of self-government, which rests in turn on the notion of the instrumental purpose of government and its institutions; the idea that institutions are made for man, not man for institutions, that in all the relationships of men— religious, political, social, and economic—those involved in and affected by decisions shall participate in their determination.

The notion of the mutually instrumental relationship of government to its people is, of course, not exclusively American. It has, however, received peculiar emphasis in American history. It marks the difference between American individualism in practice and the concept of *laissez faire*. Throughout our history, the American has turned consistently to his government for help in time of need and for the assistance requisite to keep open the roads to opportunity. And he has reserved always the right to criticize the methods government employs in meeting these needs! It is an axiom in American life that governments rest on the consent of the governed. Civil rights are indispensable conditions for maintaining the disinterested character of government functions. An instrument can serve many purposes. A government of the people may follow false gods and is peculiarly susceptible to pressure groups. For this reason channels of appeal and ready means for rectifying abuses and awakening dull consciences need ever to be at hand. And so it is, that just as the school must introduce young people to a conscious realization of worth as an element in our tradition, it must likewise inform them through precept and practice of the importance of civil rights. It should help them to grasp the fact, through the subject matter of the classroom, the practices of school government, and observation of outside events, that civil rights provide controlled methods leading to change. It is thus legitimate and necessary to use history, literature, drama, the festival to encourage an emotional identification of the individual with their establishment; to fire imagination with their significance and heighten appreciation of the sacrifices men have undergone in order to win and sustain our civil rights. Otherwise there is grave danger that hard-won gains will be exchanged for a mess of pottage.

The school, in building this conception of the relation of government and its people, should also familiarize young people with the constructive services and functions of government and thus enable them to derive both comfort and confidence from a positive insight into governmental operations at their best. This can honestly be done. The average adult knows too little about the high quality and the distinctive services rendered by many of our government departments and bureaus. All too frequently attention is occupied with the failures of government, its prostitution through political influence and special privilege. Quite a different picture of the relation of government to its citizens emerges from an intimate study of the many ways in which our governments—municipal, state, and national—minister to the varied needs of people.

A third element in the democratic tradition, necessarily associated with the attribution of worth and the instrumental function of human institutions, is an ultimate reliance on orderly, rational, and peaceful methods of resolving conflicts in interests. This is particularly significant in a democracy, which employs procedures that are consciously designed to insure changes sensitive to all the values inherent in conflicting situations.

The attempt to adjust disputes in an orderly and rational manner in a society committed to change has resulted in the evolution of the conference method. This presupposes, typically, a round table at which all interests are represented with a free hearing for all. In the course of this mutually interactive interpretation, new light is shed on issues and the participants become aware of situational elements of which they were previously unconscious. Consequently, new suggestions and new programs of action eventually emerge which in some measure meet the desires of all, solutions different from those dictated by a narrow, one-sided interest. This difference between merely voting on issues and a method which seeks to bring minds together is all important educationally and has profound implications, not merely for the conduct of the classroom, but for the administration of the school and relations within the home.

Precisely because the conference method is a democratic substitute for resort to violence, it is necessary to acquaint students with its evolution in history; to help them comprehend its wider significance, and to exemplify its operations in classroom and the life of the school. When it is so exemplified and practised as the normal method of resolving conflicts between interests, it will become virtually impossible for young people to accept the principles of an authoritarian state. But here again we must stress the point that the way of life thus lived must be generalized; students must become conscious of possible extensions of the method thus employed in the school environment to disputes outside, as for example, those between capital and labor and disputes between states.

V

We have said that schools should give reality to democratic principles through practice, and secondly, that democracy requires an ideology as well as a way of life. Obviously this bears directly upon our traditional conception of intellectual freedom concerning which we must say a concluding word.

The right to think for one's self, to arrive at one's own conclusions, and to share these conclusions with others is basic in a democracy and constitutes an invaluable method for insuring orderly change. It follows that schools and colleges are effective only when academic freedom is assured the teacher, particularly when the training of young people in the methods and techniques of accurate and responsible thinking looms large in the educational program. This is well established in the theory if not the practice of democratic education.

Oddly enough, however, far more attention has been directed toward the teacher's right to speak his mind than to his responsibility as teacher to train his students in the well-tested methods of careful thinking. Indeed, one may hazard the observation that the difficulties now encountered in assuring freedom for the teacher follow from a general assumption, unfortunately widely accepted, that education is a passive, receptive process rather than an active, creative operation of the mind in which an individual learns to shape effectively his own world.

Closely associated with this passive conception of learning is a tendency to conceive of freedom of thought as analogous to *laissez faire* in economic relations. Consequently the ideal of many teachers who seek honestly to prepare their students for participation in a free society extends no farther than to lay before them all the facts relating to a controversial issue on the assumption that by some God-given faculty the latter will arrive at decisions which are true because undictated. But *laissez faire* and the absence of guiding principles of procedure is as disastrous in thinking on economic and social and moral questions as it is inadequate as a way of living in a complex society.

Some schools have indeed realized of late a need for better guidance in thinking and have introduced propaganda analysis as one means of inoculating students against the wiles and devices of the propagandist. All of this is to the good as an act of prevention. Young people can thus acquaint themselves with fallacious operations of thought and become adept in detecting false appeals to emotion and sentiments and loyalties. But this, too, falls short of what is essential, since it is largely negative in its effects. Outcomes are often confined to an intellectual disillusionment and a suspicion of all appeals to emotion. But since the pale light of reason, unsustained by the warm blood of conviction, leads at best to feeble conclusions devoid of action, can we wonder that indifference and unconcern for the issues of life sometimes result?

Sterile outcomes in the preparation of young people for intelligent participation in democratic living derive also from recent tendencies to identify all valid thinking with the methods characteristic of the natural sciences. It is assumed that the good teacher of economics, of political science, even of the humanities, in so far as these involve problems of conduct, should imitate the disinterested method of the natural sciences, particularly their indifference to a conclusion except as this follows in an unbiased manner from data gathered and interpreted objectively.

As we have already indicated these two types of reasoning differ. The natural scientist cannot permit his preferences to determine his selection of one major premise as against another. The determining criteria are found outside his own life values. Indeed, the moment commitments of this character creep into his reasoning or his laboratory procedure, he ceases to be a genuine scientist. In the realm of social thinking, on the other hand, precisely the reverse holds true. Here it is that deep-seated preferences, one's ultimate scheme of values, the ways of life we hold most dear, constitute of necessity the major premises to which all data and all proposed solutions of specific problems are referred. The disinterestedness of the scientist applies only to the procedures that follow thereafter.

Today democracy competes with totalitarian claims for the loyalties of youth. It is therefore all-important that schools and colleges make explicit the democratic values Americans seek to live by and the ultimate criteria upon which we base the solutions of the problems of our common life. These reduce, first, to an abiding faith in the worth and the uniqueness of each individual, a respect for his integrity and his right to self-development irrespective of the accidents of birth; secondly, to the principle of mutuality in living which contrasts alike with individualism and collectivism; a conviction that self-realization is attained only when employed on behalf of the self-realization of another. Finally these principles require as a means to their adequate realization a training in the unbiased search for truth.

When the American school dedicates itself whole-heartedly to these tasks perhaps there will emerge the cultured individual of Emerson's vision:

> Can rules or tutors educate
> The semi-god whom we await?
> He must be musical,
> Tremulous, impressional,
> Alive to gentle influence
> Of landscape and of sky,
> And tender to the spirit-touch
> Of man's and maiden's eye:
> But to his native center fast,
> Shall into Future fuse the Past,
> And the world's flowing fates in
>   his own mould recast.

Index